The Everyday Calcium Cookbook:

Calcium-Rich Nutrition for Whole-Body Health

Helen Bishop MacDonald

KEY PORTER BOOKS

National Library of Canada Cataloguing in Publication

MacDonald, Helen Bishop, 1941–
    The everyday calcium cookbook : calcium-rich nutrition for whole-body health / Helen Bishop MacDonald.

Includes bibliographical references and index.
ISBN 1-55263-582-1

    1. High-calcium diet—Recipes. I. Title.

RM237.56.M33 2004   641.5'632   C2004-900385-2

The publisher gratefully acknowledges the support of the Canada Council for the Arts and the Ontario Arts Council for its publishing program. We acknowledge the support of the Government of Ontario through the Ontario Media Development Corporation's Ontario Book Initiative.

We acknowledge the financial support of the Government of Canada through the Book Publishing Industry Development Program (BPIDP) for our publishing activities.

Key Porter Books Limited
70 The Esplanade
Toronto, Ontario
Canada M5E 1R2

www.keyporter.com

Text design: Peter Maher
Electronic formatting: Jean Lightfoot Peters

Printed and bound in Canada

04 05 06 07 08 5 4 3 2 1

Contents

Acknowledgments

I would like to acknowledge the efforts of the following women, without whose help I could not have completed this book: Janie Yoon, Beth Hickey, Jennifer Woodfine, Tricia Mock, Kerry Grady-Vincent and Gail Ewan. I would also like to thank the BC Dairy Foundation for its Calcium Calculator and Info-Access for their efforts on the nutrient analysis of each recipe.

This book is dedicated to my husband Sandy, and the other men in my life: Bish, Bill, Brennan, Ryan, and Drew, who, along with my calcium intake, have helped me stand a little taller.

Introduction

The TV talk shows, morning programs, and news magazines go on and on about diet. Every one of them harps on two themes: diets don't work, and the way to successful weight loss and maintenance is through "healthy" food choices. Not bad advice—on the surface. Yet the vast majority of recommendations for a healthy diet make no mention of calcium or its major source—milk products. The magazine I'm looking at as I write makes a point of saying you could have "a little skim milk" on your cereal—but that's a significant departure from most of the advice I've heard. If people follow this advice, by 2050 we'll be in the midst of an osteoporosis epidemic far worse than we're imagining today. Currently in North America, according to national osteoporosis organizations, one in four women and one in eight men has osteoporosis. The World Health Organization predicts that by the year 2050, 25% of Asians will be afflicted with osteoporosis. (This prediction may be modified by the fact that China is undertaking a milk promotion program for its children.)

One of the questions often asked about calcium is: Why can't we just have a blood test that will tell us what we're lacking ("you're down a quart"), so we can take a pill and make everything hunky-dory? Unfortunately, it doesn't work that way. Calcium is such an important nutrient that, unless there's something seriously wrong with you, the amount in your blood is always going to be what it should be. If your diet is very low in calcium, the blood will send out a little hormonal messenger to demand that it receives an extra supply—and that supply is taken from the bones. There's a lot of talk about the bones being your calcium "bank." That's exactly what they are: a warehouse of calcium, ready to permit withdrawals when the need arises. The body does a bang-up job of making sure you have just the right amount of calcium in your blood, even if your diet is only Twinkies and Coke, but—and this is a big but—payment is extracted from your bones.

The main storage area for calcium is in the trabeculae, the ends of long bones. If the trabecular stores are all used up (which will happen if the diet is continually low in calcium), then calcium is withdrawn from the shafts of the bones to meet the body's needs. The more calcium that's taken out, the weaker the bones become.

Your challenge is to make sure you're delivering enough calcium to your body on a daily basis, so that it doesn't have to dip into its bone-bank reserves to make up for the deficit. In *The Everyday Calcium Cookbook*, I'll help you understand why calcium is so important, explain all the health problems adequate calcium can help you avoid, and tempt you with delicious, easy-to-make recipes that will ensure you're always "topped up."

1

Chapter 1

Calcium and the Nutrient Team

The human body is made up of many things—carbon, hydrogen, oxygen and nitrogen, to name a few. After these big four, calcium is the most abundant element in our personal package. Roughly 2% of the average adult's total body weight is calcium. In fact, half of all the minerals our bodies contain is pure calcium. And nearly all of that (say 99%) is found in our bones and teeth. The other 1%—no less important because of the small amount—is in blood and other body fluids. Doing what? you might well ask.

Well, for openers, seeing to the important task of blood clotting. It's thanks to calcium that, after you cut yourself, platelets are able to release thromboplastin which, also thanks to calcium, is able to activate prothromlin and cause it to change to thrombin, which then converts fibrinogen to fibrin, which makes the clot that seals the wound so you don't bleed to death. All in a day's work for calcium.

Calcium is also required for the absorption of dietary vitamin B_{12}, the regulation of muscle relaxation and contraction, the creation of a neurotransmitter called acetylcholine and the activation of many important enzymes like pancreatic lipase.

But calcium is best known for its starring role in bone development and tooth formation. The bone-building process called ossification starts in the fetus and goes into overdrive during the growing years of childhood. Ossification is essentially a "pas de deux" between cartilage and an inorganic complex of calcium, phosphorus and hydroxide ions. Together, these dance partners form bones, and the more calcium that's available, the stronger the bones will be. Throughout our lives, bone tissue is formed and destroyed in a continuous remodeling of the skeleton. It's been calculated that the total calcium content of the skeleton is replaced once every five years.

Tooth formation is not unlike bone building. It, too, begins in the fetus. Along with calcium, phosphorus, magnesium and fluorine are needed to form healthy teeth. Teeth change very little once they have erupted into the mouth as permanent teeth and have completed their mineralization. Tooth loss as we age is primarily the result of gum disease or osteoporosis in the jaw bone, which leaves the teeth with very little to which they can attach.

The importance of calcium is emphasized by the fact that blood levels of this mineral are kept within very narrow limits. The normal range of serum calcium is 9 to 11 milligrams daily. Two milligrams is not a large spread. For many nutrients there's quite a wide range between too little and too much, and nothing catastrophic happens if blood levels vary from time to time. With calcium, however, a slight dip in blood levels (hypocalcemia) results in *tetany*, a condition whereby the muscles become stiff and contracted and the nerves experience hyperactivity. If the levels of calcium in the blood are too high (hypercalcemia), calcium is deposited in soft tissues such as the heart and kidneys. This is not a good thing because it leads to plaque accumulation, especially on the arterial walls. Hypocalcemia and hypercalcemia occur, however, only when there's a foul-up in the body's calcium-regulating mechanisms, not when you consume too much or too little calcium. The body has control mechanisms that act as "gatekeepers," letting calcium in and out as needed. If you consume too much, the body excretes the excess; if you consume too little, the body simply takes calcium from your bones.

The Nutrient Team

A great deal of this book will be devoted to calcium: where to find it, what determines its absorbability (that is, how much of what you eat actually ends up in your bloodstream), how much you need, and so forth. And certainly calcium is an important—perhaps the most important—nutrient in your diet. But from my perspective as a dietitian/nutritionist, the most important thing to understand is that *calcium can't do it alone.* Healthy bones depend on teamwork. A whole slew of nutrients must work together. Calcium may be the quarterback, but it's definitely a team effort.

One of the many fascinating aspects of nutrition is the interplay between various nutrients. Most of the biochemical activity that goes on in the body—and let's face it, we're basically walking laboratories—is dependant on many nutrients, not just one. So, for example, vitamin A is important for healthy eyes, but can't be absorbed without dietary fat. Folic acid is involved in a number

Back in 526 BC the Egyptians and Persians were engaged in a serious disagreement. Tiptoeing among the corpses after one particularly gruesome battle, a victorious Egyptian officer noted that the Persian skulls were porous and fragile, while the fallen Egyptians had skulls that were strong. The Egyptian astutely observed that his men had gone bareheaded from childhood, while the Persians wore turbans as protection from the sun. We may thank the Greek historian Herodotus for this tantalizing bit of information. What we now know is that the sun exposure enabled the Egyptians to convert the precursor of vitamin D in their skin into the real McCoy, so that calcium could promote the development of strong, healthy bones. The Persians had vitamin D deficiency.

of physiological functions, but usually needs the help of vitamin B_6 and B_{12}. Calcium, depending on which task it's performing, calls on various other nutrients to lend a hand. Vitamin D is crucial, as are the minerals phosphorus and magnesium. Healthy bones won't result simply from adequate calcium in the diet; protein is needed as well. But too much protein in the face of poor calcium intake makes for other bone problems.

Vitamin D

No discussion of healthy bones, or a healthy body for that matter, would be complete without a look at the role of vitamin D. By the time calcium reaches your small intestine, it's ready to be absorbed. But it requires vitamin D to ease its transport across the intestinal mucosa.

The skin and hair of animals, including us, contain a substance called 7-dehydrocholesterol, which, in the presence of the ultraviolet rays of the sun, becomes cholecalciferol, or vitamin D_3. Vitamin D deficiency—known in childhood as rickets and in adults as osteomalacia—has been plaguing man ever since he took to wearing clothes and living in houses in the north. Rickets is known to have peaked during the Industrial Revolution, when children spent most of their waking hours toiling in factories. If they worked outdoors, the smoke from coal, wood fires and factories filtered out most of the ultraviolet light. Eventually it was discovered that, along with sunlight, cod-liver oil and butterfat prevented the disease, and the active ingredient was termed vitamin D simply because it was the fourth vitamin discovered.

Vitamin D is a fat-soluble vitamin, a fact that is important to remember when you're considering taking supplements. Because it is stored in the body's fat, a toxic build-up of vitamin D can occur. While there is a higher upper safety limit than was once thought, you *can* have too much of a good thing. You probably shouldn't exceed 2,000 IUs (international units) or 50 micrograms of vitamin D in a day, although some researchers argue for a higher intake. No such toxicity

occurs from sun exposure—you'd be burned to a crisp before that happened.

Because vitamin D is fat-soluble, anything that interferes with fat absorption will reduce the amount of vitamin D available to the body. A good example is the use of mineral oil in the treatment of constipation, which used to be a common practice among the elderly. This was most unfortunate, as many seniors have other habits that conspire to make them good candidates for vitamin D deficiency—they stay indoors a good deal of the time, and if they do go out it's hardly ever in a bikini.

While important in protecting us from skin cancer, sunscreens block the skin's ability to produce vitamin D. Data presented at a National Institute of Nutrition conference showed that even young women in their twenties and thirties have inadequate levels of vitamin D. Along with inadequate dietary intakes of the vitamin, one reason cited was the use of sunscreens. It's important to bear in mind that smoke, fog, glass and smog shield us from ultraviolet light as well. Clothing also acts as a shield from the sun, and therefore against vitamin D production. This makes for a big problem for women in parts of the Middle East whose bodies are almost completely covered. The problem is exacerbated when these women move to a country with a less sunny climate and continue to dress according to their traditions.

How Much Is Enough?

Vitamin D activity is expressed in international units (IUs), or as micrograms of cholecalciferol. One microgram equals 40 IUs. You might see a recommendation for 200 IUs or 5 micrograms. If you're confronted with a recommendation in micrograms, just multiply it by forty and you'll be in IUs. (Problems arise over the abbreviation of the word micrograms, which is µg. This sometimes appears as mg, which, of course, is milligrams—not the same thing at all.)

As of this writing, the jury is still out on how much vitamin D is enough. Certainly there are the official recommendations: it's suggested, for example, that adults up to age fifty have 400 IUs (10 µg), and beyond that 800 IUs (20 µg). However, there are some scientists who argue that even 1,000 IUs per day may not be enough, and their arguments are pretty persuasive. In addition to osteoporosis, illnesses such as colon cancer and breast cancer, among others, have been linked to inadequate supplies of vitamin D.

Where to Find It

Aside from certain fish and fish-liver oils, the only significant natural source of vitamin D is that produced by sunlight. Fortified milk is the best source in the North American diet, followed by egg yolks, butter, fish oils and organ meats. Some fish, such as cod, store their oil, and hence their vitamin D, in their livers; the flesh of the fish itself is not a great source. The "fatty fish," such as salmon, mackerel and tuna, are very good sources; unfortunately, they're not eaten as much as one (one being a dietitian) would like.

Milk is the only dairy product to which vitamin D is added. There are some yogurts, however, that are made from fortified milk—check the label. If you opt for a supplement such as cod-liver oil, remember not to overdo it. Erring on the side of caution, I'd repeat the advice not to exceed 2,000 IUs (50 µg) in a day. If you have four 8-ounce (250 mL) glasses of milk each day, you'll be getting 400 IUs.

Protein

It's one thing to make sure that you take in enough calcium, it's quite another to see that you hold on to it. Foods or nutrients that lead to excessive losses of calcium in the urine are said to have a "calciuric effect." There is a fair amount of evidence that urinary loss of calcium is greatly influenced by the amount of protein consumed in the diet: the more protein, the more calcium is excreted in the urine.

The view that large amounts of dietary protein were responsible for, or at least co-conspirators in the development of, osteoporosis came about as a result of work with the Inuit. It was found that even young Inuit men in their forties were prone to developing osteoporosis as a result of their extremely high protein intake (in the range of 11 ounces/300 grams, from whales and fish) and very low calcium consumption. Yes, an inordinate intake of protein can pose a problem, but protein is necessary for healthy bones. The rule of thumb is that for each gram of protein consumed, there is a urinary loss of one milligram of calcium. Even if you were eating 30 grams more protein than you otherwise require, your calcium losses would be insignificant—as long as your calcium intake was optimal.

Many studies have shown that people, particularly seniors, whose protein consumption is deficient, put themselves at increased risk of osteoporosis. What's really important here, however, is the calcium intake. Even if the protein intake is ideal, insufficient calcium in the diet is going to spell trouble. About the only food that delivers the ideal ratio of calcium and protein is the milk product group.

Chapter 2
Calcium for Life

It will come as no surprise that your calcium requirements change as you journey through life. Recently, as I waited in an airport lounge, I overheard a mother in her forties nagging her daughter (who looked about ten) to drink her milk. The daughter shot back, "Why aren't you drinking any?" Mom answered, "Because I'm all grown up. I don't need it." Now, put yourself in my shoes. Do I butt in? I don't want to contradict the mother in front of her child, but . . . she does still need it. Her requirements are just different from her daughter's.

In the end I wimped out of speaking up, but the woman's comment speaks to a widely held belief that consumption of milk products is important only in childhood and pregnancy. An old milk commercial stated that you never outgrow your need for milk. For real accuracy we should say that you never out grow your need for calcium—milk is just a handy vehicle for delivering it. In the next few sections we'll see just how our age affects our basic calcium needs.

TABLE 1
Canada's Food Guide to Healthy Eating

Recommended daily servings of milk products

Children 4–9 years	2–3 servings/day
Youth 10–16 years	3–4 servings/day
Adults	2–4 servings/day
Pregnant and breast-feeding women	3–4 servings/day

Calcium Intake in Childhood

The average 7½-pound newborn has a little over an ounce (roughly 32 grams) of calcium in its bones. During the first couple of years of life, calcium intake is critical. Daily calcium intake should be around 20 mg per pound of body weight (44 per kg). So, a 20-pound baby would need approximately 400 mg of calcium every day. Since milk forms the major part of the diet in infancy, calcium needs are readily met, along with those of other vital nutrients.

As the baby eases into childhood, the growth rate subsides somewhat, and so does the proportional need for calcium. Up until about age ten, the daily intake of calcium should be more in the area of 10 mg per pound—generally about 800 mg.

When adolescence hits, it's time to get really serious about dietary calcium. Unfortunately, especially for adolescent girls, calcium isn't usually a top priority. Poor bone development in adolescence is sure to spell trouble in later years, but it's a very rare teenager who gives any thought to the seventy-year-old she'll one day be. Teens—both male and female—need 1,200 mg to 1,400 mg of calcium per day, every day.

A child's bone health largely depends on his parents: genetics plays a big part, but so does the kind of diet they provide him with in childhood. Malnourished children do not fare well, either physically or intellectually. The term "malnourished" conjures up a picture of a child with toothpick limbs and a distended belly; that type of situation doesn't exist in North America, right? Not for the vast majority, but for a growing number of children micronutrient deficiency is an increasing problem. The reasons vary, from the time-pressed two-income household with little time for traditional meal preparation, to campaigns by animal-rights activists to convince parents that meat and dairy products are dangerous for their children, to simple nutritional ignorance in a culture seduced by the thought that overfed equals well-fed.

To explore the question of why diet matters to a developing child, we must ask what the nutritional status and probable physical, medical and intellectual outcomes would be for a child whose diet contained no milk or milk products. For the sake of argument, let's assume that, aside from having nothing from the milk group, the child's diet met all of the other recommendations from the *U.S. Food Pyramid* or *Canada's Food Guide to Healthy Eating*. (This is a highly speculative assumption given current eating patterns, but let's pretend.) Recent studies have shown that vegan children (who consume no animal foods, including milk or milk products) had significantly impaired cognitive abilities compared to a control group of similarly aged children following a balanced, four-food-group diet. What might explain this difference in abilities? Well, subclinical vitamin B_{12} deficiency is associated with diminished mental acuity in both adolescents and the elderly. Furthermore, while it's well-established that animal foods are the only source of vitamin B_{12} (unless you count bacterial production on produce contaminated with cow manure), research has now shown

that the vitamin B_{12} from milk is significantly more bioavailable (which simply means that more of it makes its way from your stomach to your bloodstream to be available to the body) than that from other animal foods. Vitamin B_{12}, of course, is only one of many nutrients in milk that helps to nourish the brain, but it's an extremely important one.

Now consider the impact of a milk-free diet on bone health and long-term maintenance. Adolescent girls are particularly vulnerable. Roughly 40% of their bone density is acquired during puberty—less dietary calcium equals lower bone mass. In the short term, this lower bone mineral density translates to increased incidence of forearm fractures. And active teenage girls who drink carbonated soft drinks have been found to be more likely to break a bone than girls at the same level of activity that don't drink the carbonated beverages. The long-term consequences are potentially catastrophic. Osteoporosis has been characterized as a juvenile disease that's manifested in the elderly. What this means is that the stage is set for the condition while we are still young. Consuming insufficient calcium means that we don't achieve "peak bone mass." That is, we don't build the maximum amount of bone that our genes would dictate. Then, when we become elderly, we have less bone matter than we should have. Bone loss occurs, and osteoporosis is the result. Most young men are big consumers of calcium, so they develop pretty good bones as adolescents. Girls are another story, however, and the mature women they will one day become are quite apt to rue the dietary choices they made as teens.

While it's not impossible for a child on a milk-free diet to obtain all the nutrients needed for bone growth and health, it is difficult in the extreme, and in today's soda-pop culture, highly unlikely. Milk and milk products are not the only sources of calcium, but they're far ahead of all the other sources. A case can be made for the calcium content of sardines, kale and bok choy, but even children who love these foods are not likely to eat them three times a day.

What about beverages fortified with calcium—won't they help a child get the necessary calcium? Sure they'll help, but unfortunately calcium can't carry the responsibility for healthy bones all on its own. Bone growth and maintenance depend upon many nutrients and, as it turns out, milk is the only food that naturally contains them all. This is an agricultural practice that has been used for 10,000 years—Mother Nature had a pretty good plan when she determined that humans could use mammalian milk for their own sustenance. Dr. Lynn McIntyre, Dean of Health Sciences at Dalhousie University, who has just completed a study on the health and nutritional status of economically deprived women and children, found that "For those children, the one food that could spell the difference in meeting their nutritional needs or not—that one food is milk."

There are many excellent books about childhood nutrition that cover, among other things, requirements for calcium, vitamin D and all of the other nutrients that make for a healthy infant and child. My suggestions in the Bibliography at the back of the book give excellent recommendations about dietary patterns and lifestyles.

Calcium and the Healthy Adult

Peak bone mass is pretty well established by age twenty, and no significant loss begins for a couple of decades. But remember that bone matter is completely replaced about every five years. The stuff is *living*.

Imagine the worst diet you can think of, let's say a donut and soft drink for breakfast, French fries and gravy for lunch, and a couple of jelly sandwiches for dinner. (Don't laugh—one of my son's roommates actually tried to survive on a plan like this.) There's next to no calcium. In fact, almost no nutrients at all, aside from the vitamins added to the donut and bread, and some vitamin C and potassium in the fries. What's the body going to do to get the calcium it needs? The blood absolutely has to have calcium to perform its essential functions (as discussed in Chapter 1), so it sends out a hormonal messenger to the bones demanding that calcium be supplied right away. And the calcium is withdrawn from the bone bank.

Now, the diet I've described is an exaggeration—most people eat better than that. But I hope the point is clear: if you don't have enough calcium in your diet in early adulthood, your bones will make up the deficit, and that will mean lower bone density at the start of your senior years, when osteoporosis rears its ugly head. Let's assume you follow the same calcium-deficient diet for thirty years. Every day, day after day, because your diet is low in calcium, withdrawals are made from your bones to meet the blood's constant demand for calcium. Thirty years of withdrawals are bound to make a dent. But the bigger your bank account, the longer it takes before you need to declare bankruptcy.

The less bone mass you have to begin with, the sooner you'll develop osteoporosis.

A frequent question concerns men's lower risk of osteoporosis. After all, if osteoporosis is partly the result of decreased estrogen production in women, and men are never big estrogen producers, they should have higher rates of osteoporosis, not lower. Maybe men aren't high on the estrogen scale, but they do produce testosterone. Hormones aside, however, the issue has more to do with how large and dense your bones are before you start losing bone mass. Men, in general, have denser bones to begin with. But a man who lives long enough on a calcium-deficient diet will develop osteoporosis.

Calcium and the Pregnant Woman

It has been suggested, and there is some research to back it up, that the pregnant woman's ability to absorb calcium is somewhat increased during this time. That's a good thing, since almost every day of the last three months of pregnancy sees a whopping 300 mg of calcium deposited in the baby's skeleton.

Calcium is extremely important to a developing fetus, especially for bone development and tooth formation. The tooth-making process begins about four months into the pregnancy and resembles bone formation in a variety of ways: calcium and phosphorus (along with magnesium and fluoride) mineralize a protein matrix to give teeth their rigidity.

The fetus won't pay the price if Mom's diet is low in calcium. Mom will. All the calcium going into the production of the baby has to come from somewhere, and if it's not in the diet, it will be taken out of the mother's bones, including her jawbone and teeth. Unlike bone calcium, tooth calcium can't be replaced once it's been lost. There used to be an expression "for every child, a tooth," because with improper diet and dental care, a woman's jawbone can be so weakened in pregnancy that she loses one or more teeth.

Calcium and the Golden Years

The thought has been expressed that having lots of calcium in the diet once one has become a "senior" is a bit like locking the barn door after the horse is gone. Not so. While it is true that the ideal is to get all the calcium necessary during adolescence, adequate dietary calcium is important throughout life. And not just to reduce the risk of osteoporosis, as we'll soon see. But for now let's focus on that crippling disease, and the role that calcium plays in helping to avoid it.

Evidence of osteoporosis has been found in prehistoric skeletons dating as far back as 2000 BC. The term comes from the Latin words *osteo*, meaning bone, and *porous*, meaning holey—holey bones. Technically, the condition is said to exist when over one-third of the bone is lost. Between the ages of thirty and forty, women can lose roughly 10% of their bone mass—men about 3%—and the same again in each subsequent decade. But even though we all lose bone mass as we age, we don't all develop osteoporosis. We're not sure exactly why some people are slow losers while others are rapid losers, nor do we understand why some lose more in the spine, others in the hips and still others in the femurs.

Naturally, loss of bone matrix and mineral leaves us more susceptible to fracture or breakage. You've perhaps heard of an older woman who was walking across the kitchen floor, fell and broke a hip. Just as likely a scenario is that she was walking across the kitchen floor, broke a hip, then fell. These "spontaneous" fractures, which result from little or no trauma, happen with alarming frequency. People can and do die from the complications of bone fractures, and if they don't die, their quality of life is seriously altered—often it's the sole reason that a woman has to enter a nursing home. The cost to the health care system is enormous.

Sometimes osteoporosis results in compression of the vertebrae, which causes chronic back pain and difficulty in getting around. When the vertebrae are weakened or compressed, a deformity of the spine, known medically as kyphosis, but referred to by most of us as "dowager's hump," occurs. It's these compressions of the vertebrae that lead to the loss of height we see in so many older women.

There are many excellent books devoted entirely to osteoporosis and its treatment, as well as excellent information available from osteoporosis associations. You'll find some recommendations in the Bibliography at the end of this book. My aim is to help ensure that your diet is adequate in calcium so that you'll reduce your risk of osteoporosis and the other conditions associated with poor calcium intake (see Chapter 5).

Chapter 3

How Much Calcium Is Enough?

What is the optimal amount of calcium to keep your bones movin' and jivin,' carrying you through a healthy adulthood and into the golden years? As is true of most of nutrition, it ain't that simple. Well, yes, we have "official recommendations" (see Table 1). But we have to take a couple of things into consideration when determining just how much calcium is enough.

The initial recommendations for calcium intake were based on a typical mixed diet—a balanced intake of each of the food groups. The experts understood (then and now) that not all of the calcium in all foods reaches the bloodstream with the same level of efficiency. We're talking about "bioavailability," the phenomenon whereby what you see (in terms of nutrients) isn't necessarily what you get. Substances called anti-nutrients reduce the amount of a nutrient that the body can absorb. In the case of calcium, some of those anti-nutrients are a couple of nasties called oxalic acid and phytic acid.

Oxalates are found primarily in vegetables, while phytates are found in whole grains and legumes. Both combine with minerals calcium and iron, and form an insoluble salt that the body simply can't absorb. So all that talk you've heard about green leafy vegetables being a great source of calcium applies only to a select group of greens: broccoli, bok choy and kale. In terms of calcium, spinach is practically useless. Same goes for Swiss chard. Don't get me wrong, these are great veggies for things like beta-carotene and potassium, but their content of oxalic acid makes them a distinctly unreliable source of calcium. You also shouldn't count on grains as a major source of calcium, even whole grains such as whole wheat bread and whole cereal. Foods rich in fiber are generally praised—as well they should be—but not only do they contain phytic acid, the fiber itself can reduce the absorption of calcium.

As I mentioned, the original calcium recommendations were based on a mixed diet. What if you adopt a vegetarian diet? If your diet involves the exclusion of meat, fish, poultry and eggs, but includes milk products, while you face problems with iron, zinc and other minerals, you could be okay in terms of calcium. Better, in fact, if you're relying on dairy for your protein. Most studies have shown that the bone health of balanced lacto-vegetarians and omnivores is about equal. Trouble pops up if you consume only foods from the plant kingdom because, as we've seen, the bioavailability issue makes it almost impossible for the body to get all the calcium it needs from unfortified plant foods alone. The strictly vegan diet puts other nutrients at risk as well, including vitamins B_{12} and D. The bottom line is that if the best sources of calcium (milk products) are not in the diet, supplements are needed.

Where to Find It

We've touched on bioavailability already—you understand that calcium isn't an equal-opportunity nutrient. But how then do we decide which foods are excellent sources of calcium, which are very good, which are so-so and so on. Well, there is a formula. To begin with, nutrition scientists have calculated the bioavailability of most foods that are contenders in the calcium sweepstakes. For example, milk has a bioavailability factor of 32%, which means that for every cup (250 mL or one serving, containing about 315 mg of calcium) of milk you drink, your body will get 315 mg × 0.32 or roughly 100 mg of calcium.

Broccoli, on the other hand, has a bioavailability factor of 52%, which would seem to make it a winner, hands down. Not so fast. The *absolute* calcium content of a half cup (125 mL or one serving) of broccoli is only 50 mg, so 50 mg × 0.52 equals 26 mg of calcium. It would take four times as much broccoli to deliver the same amount of calcium that milk gives. You get the picture. A food's value as a source of calcium is dependent on two things: how much calcium it actually contains (its absolute content) and its bioavailability factor. To make it easier, here's a chart showing how much of various foods you'd have to eat to absorb the same amount of calcium in 1 cup (250 mL) of milk.

TABLE 2

Food	Approximate serving size
Almonds	³/₄ cup (175 mL)
Baked beans	2 cups (500 mL)
Bok choy, cooked	2 cups (500 mL)
Brazil nuts	1¹/₄ cups (300 mL)
Bread, whole wheat or white	13 slices
Broccoli, cooked	4 cups (1 L)
Chickpeas, cooked	3³/₄ cups (875 mL)
Chili con carne	4¹/₂ cups (1.125 L)
Collards, cooked	2 cups (500 mL)
Dates	5¹/₂ cups (1.375 L)
Figs, dried	12
Kale, cooked	3¹/₄ cups (800 mL)
Lentils, cooked	8 cups (2 L)
Nuts, mixed	3 cups (750 mL)
Orange	5¹/₂ medium
Prunes, dried, uncooked	80
Raisins	3³/₄ cups (875 mL)
Red kidney beans, cooked	6 cups (1.5 L)
Rice, white or brown, cooked	15³/₄ cups (3.925 L)
Salmon, pink, canned, with bones	³/₄ of a 213 g can
Salmon, sockeye, canned, with bones	⁵/₈ of a 213 g can

Sardines, canned with bones	*7 medium (83 g)*
Sesame seeds	*1¾ cups (425 mL)*
Soybeans, cooked	*1¾ cups (425 mL)*
Soy beverage	*31½ cups (7.875 L)*
Soy beverage, fortified	*1 cup (250 mL)*
Tofu, regular, processed with calcium sulfate	*⅔ cups (200 g)*
White beans, cooked	*1¾ cups (425 mL)*

Source: Adapted from The Calcium Content of Other Foods in the Dairy Farmers of Canada's brochure "Calcium for Life: Are You on the Right Track?" Used with permission.

There are a few foods, well one anyway, that's an even better source of calcium than milk—sardines! But make sure you get the kind that still has the bones in them. I remember the first time I saw sardines with the bones removed. I thought, "Is nothing sacred?" Too bad people don't eat them more often, since sardines are also a great source of vitamin D.

Some foods that need attention are not on the table. There has been some concern that the oxalic acid in chocolate milk reduces the bioavailability of the milk's calcium. As in many nutrition myths, there's a kernel of truth here. Yes, there is some oxalic acid in the chocolate, but it is so little as to make it inconsequential. Instead of 315 mg of calcium in a glass, you'd get only about 310 mg. Another puzzlement surrounds soy beverages: when you check out the calcium content of soy beverages in any of the reliable nutrient value tables, you see that it has only 10 mg of calcium per cup (250 mL). Yet soy beverages are often cited as an excellent source of calcium. That's because calcium along with other nutrients, is added in the manufacturing process, in an effort at making it as nutritious as milk. (Calcium-fortified juices also have a calcium supplement added to them.) This undoubtedly adds to the calcium content, but as I said earlier, calcium can't do it alone. Because of soy's inferior bioavailability (25% less than that of milk), I cannot recommend it as a complete alternative.

Supplements—When Diet Isn't Enough

Let's face it, as much as I and most dietitians would like to believe that everybody follows the ideal diet, balanced with all the food groups, there are times when and people for whom this just isn't going to happen. I'll confine myself to the milk and milk products group for this discussion. Some people just don't get enough. The reasons are many and varied, from the simple case of those who just don't like milk, through misconceptions about lactose intolerance, all the way to wrong-headed ideas about weight control. The fact is that the average North American woman barely gets one full serving of milk products per day. That gives her about 300 mg of calcium, and the rest of her diet, if it's made up of healthful choices, will donate another 300 mg. So she has an average intake of 600 mg—tops. Compare that to the 1,000 mg minimum recommended, and you can see that we're headed for trouble.

And that's where supplements come in. No matter what the reason (and I'll try and explain away some of them shortly), if you're not getting sufficient calcium in your diet, you need to be taking a supplement. Use the tables in the book, along with the Calcium Calculator (see pages 15–19), and do the math. If you're supposed to be getting 1,200 mg per day and you're only consuming 300 mg, then you've got some making up to do. You can resolve to improve your diet, or you can take supplements. If you decide on the latter, then you have to bear in mind that the supplement is giving you only the calcium. Or if you take a combo pill that gives you, say, calcium, vitamin D and magnesium, then those are the nutrients you're getting. Nothing more. Yes, the calcium is important, but calcium (or calcium and a couple of friends) can't do it alone. The magic, if you will, of healthy bones seems to be found in the combination of nutrients that are found in milk products. An overwhelming amount of evidence exists that (all other things being equal) those who consume milk and milk products have better bones than those who don't. And they are also more likely to meet their requirements for other nutrients.

I'll cite just one study, but there are many, many more. This study, by Devine, Prince and Bell, was published in the 1996 *American Journal of Clinical Nutrition* and is titled "Nutritional Impact of Calcium Supplementation by Skim Milk Powder or Calcium Tablet on Total Nutrient Intake in Postmenopausal Women." Devine and his group found that the women taking "supplemental" milk powder (that is, supplemental to their regular diet) not only improved their calcium intake, but made a

significant increase in their intake of eleven other nutrients to boot.

Despite a boatload of evidence that the consumption of milk and milk products is beneficial, especially for women, we know that the per capita consumption of these foods has declined over the last twenty years. Writing in the *American Journal of Clinical Nutrition* (1996), Dr. Robert Heaney, one of the world's leading authorities on bone health, stated: "This change has many roots: a shift from milk to soft drinks; failure of a fragmented milk industry to cope in a timely fashion with shifting market forces; the growing fashion of milk-bashing and its ability to generate media coverage; the misperception that milk is intrinsically high in fat and that the low-fat varieties are low in other nutrients as well; and at the level of nutritional practitioners, a notable defeatist attitude toward encouraging increased milk consumption and a too-easy acceptance of supplements."

You don't need to be a nutrition scientist to figure out that it's best to get your nutrients from food. Having said that, however, I'll repeat what I said earlier—some people need to take a supplement. Now you need to choose the right one. You've done the math and figured out that you need 600 mg of calcium per day. You're in the calcium section at the drug store, and you're overwhelmed with the choices. Really, there's just one thing to concern yourself with (actually there are two: the supplement should have some vitamin D as well). The thing to look for on the label is the amount of *elemental* calcium in the pill. That means how much of the weight of the pill is actual calcium, not pill filler. A pill might weigh 600 mg, but some of that weight could be the stuff that's holding the calcium together. You want to know how much calcium you'll be getting when you take that pill. After that, you'll notice terms like calcium lactate, calcium gluconate, calcium carbonate or calcium citric malate. There's not a whole lot of difference, except that the lactates and gluconates are somewhat less absorbable, and the citric malates are more so. Calcium carbonate is probably a good choice, and Tums does indeed give you what it says it will.

What about the time of day you take your supplement? Does it matter? Generally, it's thought that nighttime is better, and that taking your supplement with food will increase its chances of being absorbed. (I still think you'd be better off taking a glass of warm milk with a bit of vanilla or chocolate tossed in, but you're the best judge of what works for you.)

Soy and Other Fortified Products

There are a number of products that have calcium added to them in an attempt to bring them up to the nutritional value of milk. We'll have a look at some of them.

Soy beverage on its own, that is, the liquid extracted from soy beans and processed to remove the anti-nutrients found in them, is a very poor source of calcium, with only 10 mg per a 1-cup (250 mL) serving. Some manufacturers have added calcium to their soy drinks, and some have added other nutrients to try and make a similar product to milk. Tofu, if it is set with calcium sulphate, makes a reasonable calcium contribution, but not all tofu is set with calcium. Some are set with magnesium. Read the label to be sure.

Are soy and soy products helpful in reducing the risk or incidence of osteoporosis? The fact is, we don't know. One of the common myths about osteoporosis is that the Japanese don't get it. Compounding the myth is the notion that they don't get it because their diet contains a lot of soy. Actually, Japanese women suffer from the crippling disease at rates that equal or surpass those of Caucasian women in North America: they have more osteoporosis in their spines, we have hip fractures. The hip problem is thought to be related to genetic differences in the structure of the hip.

The idea that soy might be helpful for symptoms of menopause has been pretty much discounted as well, with most scientific studies showing no effect. If, however, you consume a soy beverage fortified with calcium, you will definitely get the calcium. This is true of fortified orange juice as well. The problem is that healthy bones depend on more than just calcium, and the only food that delivers all of the necessary nutrients is milk. It's possible that soy protein, if consumed in large amounts, has a role to play in heart health, but that's a topic for another book.

The Calcium Calculator

Source: Adapted from the BC Dairy Foundation's brochure "The Calcium Calculator." Used with permission.

The calcium calculator will help you figure out just how much calcium you're getting on a given day.

Step 1

1. Check off the calcium-rich foods you ate yesterday on the chart below

(make photocopies, so you can do this every day).

2. Write the number of portions you ate for each food checked.

3. Total the number of portions, and multiply by the milligrams of calcium per portion.

4. Enter the amount in the last column.

5. Add the amounts in the last column to get your calcium intake.

Calcium-Rich Foods	Usual Portion Size	Number of Portions Yesterday	Milligrams of Calcium per Portion	Total mg of Calcium
Bread	2 slices	_____		
Broccoli, cooked	3/4 cup (175 mL)	_____		
Kidney beans, lima beans, lentils	1 cup (250 mL)	_____		
Orange (fruit not juice)	1 medium	_____		
Tahini	2 tbsp (25 mL)	_____		
	Total Portions	_____	**x 50**	= _____ mg
Bok choy or kale, cooked	1/2 cup (125 mL)	_____		
Chickpeas	1 cup (250 mL)	_____		
Cottage Cheese*	1/2 cup (125 mL)	_____		
Ice cream	1/2 cup (125 mL)	_____		
Parmesan cheese	1 tbsp (15 mL)	_____		
Almonds	1/4 cup (50 mL)	_____		
	Total Portions	_____	**x 75**	= _____ mg
Baked beans, soybeans, white beans	1 cup (250 mL)	_____		
Ice milk, frozen yogurt*	1/2 cup (125 mL)	_____		
Pancakes or waffles, made with milk	3 medium	_____		
Pudding, made with milk	1/2 cup (125 mL)			
Soft and semi-soft	1 1/4" (3 cm) cube			

Calcium-Rich Foods	Usual Portion Size	Number of Portions Yesterday	Milligrams of Calcium per Portion	Total mg of Calcium
cheese such as feta, mozzarella, camembert*				
Soup, made with milk	1 cup (250 mL)			
Tofu, made with calcium	3 oz (90 g)	_____		
	Total Portions	_____	x 150	= _____ mg
Firm cheese such as Gouda, Swiss, cheddar*	1¼" (3 cm) cube	_____		
Processed cheese slices*	2 slices	_____		
Salmon, canned with bones	½ can	_____		
Sardines, canned with bones	½ can	_____		
**Yogurt, fruit flavored*	¾ cup (175 mL)	_____		
	Total Portions	_____	x 250	= _____ mg
**Milk—skim, 1%, 2%, whole, buttermilk or chocolate	1 cup (250 mL)	_____		
Calcium-fortified beverages (e.g. soy, rice)	1 cup (250 mL)	_____		
Skim milk powder	⅓ cup (75 mL)			
**Yogurt, plain*	¾ cup (175 mL)			
	Total Portions	_____	x 300	= _____ mg

*Regular or low fat.

** Add 100 mg for each portion of calcium-enriched milk or yogurt.

Step 2

Compare your calcium intake to your recommended daily intake.

My Calcium Intake	My Recommended Intake
(from step 1)	(from chart below)

Age	Adequate Daily Intake
1–3 years	500 mg
4–8 years	800 mg
9–18 years	1,300 mg
19–50 years	1,000 mg
50+ years	1,500 mg

Did you get enough calcium? If yes, great! You're on track! If no, you need to increase your calcium intake.

These figures are from The Osteoporosis Society of Canada. The current recommendation from The National Academy of Sciences for people over 50 is 1,200 mg.

Increasing Your Intake

So let's suppose that you've figured out that your daily calcium requirement is 1,200 mg. That would be the equivalent of a balanced diet (300 mg) plus three servings of milk or milk products per day. Milk products refer to cheese, yogurt and even ice cream. A serving of yogurt would be one of those individual containers (¾ cup or 175 g). A serving of cheese would be about 2 ounces (50 g), or a piece the size of your index and middle fingers together. One and a half cups (375 mL) of ice cream would give you almost 300 mg of calcium, along with 400 calories—you make your choices!

Personally, my calcium requirements are in the 1,200 mg range. As you can well imagine, it would be really embarrassing for me to get osteoporosis. So naturally, I do all I can to prevent it, especially in terms of diet. Since I catch the train at 6:50 am every morning, I don't have time for a three-course breakfast. But I do have a great husband who whips me up a smoothie as I'm getting dressed (for great smoothie recipes, see pages 119–127). It's a four-cup concoction of yogurt, milk and fruit (fresh or frozen, depending on the season). I drink two cups before I leave the house, and the rest on the drive to the train. Then I usually have some cheese sometime during the day.

Here are some tips for adding calcium to your menu:

- Sprinkle some grated cheese over pasta dishes, salads and soups.
- Add some skim milk powder to casseroles, puddings and soups.
- Use yogurt as a topping for desserts and soups.
- Use milk instead of water in reconstituting canned soups.
- Toss shredded kale into your mixed green salad.
- Mix toasted, slivered almonds or sesame seeds with your salads, or use it as a coating on fish.
- Don't remove the bones from canned salmon—they're soft and can be easily mixed in with the fish.
- Melt cheese over vegetables like broccoli and cauliflower; this not only increases the calcium content, it also increases the likelihood that the veggies will be eaten.

- Don't sneer at cheese slices, Cheese Whiz or Velveeta—they're a surprisingly good source of calcium.
- Create some of the delicious recipes in this book!

It doesn't seem all that difficult, does it? But unless you're consciously tending to your daily calcium intake by preparing dishes that are rich in calcium, it's easy to end each day on the short end of the stick. And it's been shown time and again that the average household is in a recipe rut, with no more than ten recipes rotated routinely. The recipes in this book will help insure that your calcium bank account is always in the black.

Chapter 4
Fat and Calcium and Other Weighty Issues

I think I can safely state that one of the first things that a woman—or a man, for that matter—does upon starting a weight-loss program is to reduce or abandon milk and milk products, if there were any in their diet to begin with. The reasoning is pretty straight forward: this stuff has calories; it's not one of my big weaknesses anyway (except, perhaps, for cheese) and milk is an easy thing to give up. On the other hand, there are diet soft drinks: no calories, refreshing, no guilt. It's a no-brainer. Except that the big brains in the nutrition business have proven that there are two major flaws with this line of reasoning.

1. Dieters Lose Bone Mass

It's been shown in study after study that the average dieter comes out of her foray into slimness with less bone matter than she began with. One of the few advantages to carrying around extra weight is that it applies sufficient stress to the bones to strengthen them. In theory, the heftier you are, the stronger your bones are. Conversely, then, less heft, less bone mass. But that's only part of it. As I've said, aside from diets undertaken with the aid of a few respected weight-loss programs (Weight Watchers comes to mind), the average organized or disorganized attempt at weight loss almost invariably includes a

significant drop in calcium intake. A number of weight-loss programs recommend skim milk in the diet plan, but not many get-slim-quick schemes make room for sardines or cheese. A few will mention the benefits of kale and bok choy, and some will even praise the calcium-richness of various nuts—but because nuts contain a lot of fat, they're out.

One of the inherent problems with low-fat diets involves the "satiety value," dietitian-speak for a food's ability to help you feel full. Among a number of possible benefits, fat stays with you longer, making it less likely that hunger pangs will force you to fall off the wagon of calorie-deprived righteousness.

Which brings us to the question of skim milk versus whole milk. The vast majority of health professionals would recommend skim milk (or it's less worthy cousin, 1%), whether a person is trying to lose weight or not. They're convinced (and, to be fair, there's research to support their conviction) that the saturated fat in whole milk and 2% is a one-way ticket to heart disease. In my opinion, the average woman's intake of one cup (250 mL) of milk per day hardly warrants all the angst. We're talking about 0.2 ounces (6 grams) of saturated fatty acids instead of 0.07 ounces (2 grams), not all of which elevate serum cholesterol. Some of the saturated fat raises the good cholesterol, HDL (high-density lipoprotein). The satiety value of whole milk is completely ignored. Yet, there is pretty good evidence that a diet that includes three glasses of whole milk each day is more likely to be stuck to than one that recommends only beverages with a lower satiety value.

2. Higher Calcium Intake Leads to Better Weight Loss

Starting in about 1998, studies began to appear that showed that obese people, as a rule, had less calcium in their diet than those people of optimum or healthy body weight. These findings were a bit at odds with the stereotypical image of the overweight, scoffing back ice-cream sundaes, pizzas and fettuccini alfredo. But like much stereotyping, this misses the point. Yes, those foods may be calcium-rich (except for the alfredo), but the calcium-rich elements were combined with other high-energy sources. Not only did the studies find that people who consumed less calcium tended to be more overweight than their milk-drinking counterparts, they also exhibited greater weight gain at middle age. The battle of the bulge was bulgier for the low-calcium consumers.

Then the researchers got serious. "Suppose," they thought, "we put people on diet plans that are identical in calorie content, but significantly different in the amount of calcium they contain. Would their weight losses differ?" What do you know, the high-calcium group lost more weight. I hasten to add that this was no magic bullet. The improved weight loss was only evident when people were consuming less energy than they expended, but the results were impressive and definitive: if you're going to put your

efforts into a calorie-reduced diet, the payback will be much greater if you ensure an adequate calcium intake in the area of 1,000 mg per day.

Researchers, particularly Dr. Michael Zemel of the University of Tennessee, have theorized that having more calcium in the diet makes it less likely that the cells will store fat, and more likely that they'll be inclined to burn fat in the face of calorie deprivation. Conversely, less calcium brings about changes in cellular makeup that result in less fat burning, more fat storing. Who knew?

The upshot of all this is that people make a huge mistake when they opt for fewer calcium-rich foods in their weight-loss plan. And I'm not suggesting, nor does the research so far suggest, that the dietary calcium has to come from milk products— sardines and kale might be just as effective. What the evidence does highlight, however, is that calcium from food is much more effective than calcium from supplements. Dr. Angelo Tremblay's group at Laval University in Quebec City has published confirming evidence of the calcium connection, and these scientists suspect that perhaps calcium somehow curbs the appetite. Time will tell just how calcium works to ease the quest for a healthy weight, but there seems to be no doubt that it does.

Dairy Fat and Heart Health

Some readers might be concerned about the amount of fat in some of the recipes in this book—especially since much of the fat is of animal origin and therefore includes the dread "saturated fat." A little discussion of the facts as we now know them is in order.

To label fats "saturated," "polyunsaturated," or "monounsaturated" is misleading. Every fat or oil we eat is made up of a combination of these three types of fatty acids. Moreover, to label all saturated fatty acids as "bad" or as the cause of elevated cholesterol levels is a huge mistake.

This terminology probably started out innocently enough—a way of simplifying a complicated message for the consumer. Unfortunately, the consumer was left with a flawed message. Sure enough, there are some saturated fatty acids in animal fat that will raise the "bad" or LDL (low-density lipoprotein) cholesterol; others, however, are either neutral or even lower serum cholesterol levels. Still others are responsible for elevating the "good" cholesterol, HDL (high-density lipoprotein) . Many nutrition scientists now believe that animal fat, in moderation, is most likely neutral in terms of heart disease. Many studies have shown, in fact, that consumers of whole milk have a lower incidence of heart disease than those who drink either no milk, or fat-reduced milk and milk products. If you're interested in learning more about this view of animal fats and heart disease, check the Bibliography at the end of the book under "Calcium and Heart Disease."

To further complicate the issue, we have the emergence of research in a component of dairy fat, found in the fat of all ruminants (cud-chewing animals), called conjugated linoleic acid, or CLA for short. While there have been no long-term clinical trials on humans, animal research and epidemiological studies have shown that this substance increases resistance to various cancers. Conversely, it's also been shown that linoleic acid, found abundantly in vegetable oils, actually increases the risk of cancer when consumed in large amounts. Talk about irony: in the name of reducing heart disease, people have been urged to reduce their intake of a food now known to reduce cancer risk, while at the same time being urged to replace it with one that increases their risk. Recommending the consumption of margarine in place of butter was without a doubt ill-founded advice. Margarine, as we now know, contains trans fatty acids that not only raise the bad cholesterol, but lower the good.

Well, then, what about calories? No doubt about it, an eight-ounce (250 mL) glass of whole milk contains 68 more calories than a similar glass of skim or fat-free milk. And, despite what you might read elsewhere, calories do count. As mentioned above, however, having some fat in the food you eat helps you feel full for longer and therefore makes you disinclined to overeat. Common sense would dictate that if you're choosing a food or recipe that is higher in fat, and therefore higher in calories, you should eat smaller portions of it. You don't need to be a nutrition scientist to figure that one out.

Childhood Obesity

According to a study published in the March 2001 *Archives of Pediatric and Adolescent Medicine*, the percentage of children between eight and sixteen years of age considered obese in the United States has doubled in less than thirty years. The statistics are similarly startling for Canadian children. A study in the *Lancet* looked at the impact of children's soft-drink consumption habits on body weight, and the results were not comforting. Of those

TABLE 4

Percentage of the Recommended Daily Intake of Selected Vitamins and Minerals Available in 1-cup (250 mL) Servings of Popular Beverages

	2% Milk	Soft Drinks	Bottled Water
Vitamin A	11%	0%	0%
Vitamin C	3%	0%	0%
Vitamin D	44%	0%	0%
Riboflavin	25%	0%	0%
Folic acid	6%	0%	0%
Calcium	29%	0%	3%
Cost	$1.00	$1.00	$1.00

children who were not obese at the beginning of the study, those who were obese at the end were highly likely to have increased their intake of sugar-sweetened drinks.

Obviously, soft drinks are not the only factor in childhood obesity, but they undoubtedly play a role. There is great concern among nutritionists and dietitians that consumption of soft drinks is crowding out more nutritious choices such as milk and fruit juice. Data from the 1994–96 Continuing Survey of Food Intakes by Individuals indicate that kids who drink nutrient-poor soft drinks—64% of school-age children and 83% of adolescents—may do so at the expense of drinking more nutritious beverages. Intakes of milk nutrients and fruit juice nutrients were shown to be significantly lower in those with the highest soft drink consumption.

Research has demonstrated that consumption of milk is more than 30% lower in schools that sell soft drinks and flavored drinks in vending machines. They've also shown that children who consume soft drinks average one less serving of milk each and every day. Across all age groups, milk con-

sumption was strongly associated with the likelihood of meeting intake requirements for vitamins A and B_{12}, folate, calcium and magnesium. One doesn't need to be a nutritional scientist to realize that, unless a kid is a two-fisted drinker, the likelihood of milk and pop each having equal prominence in the diet is pretty slim.

Have a look at the nutritional bang for the buck that a child gets when choosing milk, cola or, as is becoming trendy, bottled water. See Table 4.

I should point out that not only do these soft drinks provide no nutrients, many of them make a hefty contribution of caffeine. Colas are the worst, but not the only offenders. In a small body, a can of caffeinated cola is equal to about four cups of coffee in an adult. With excessive caffeine intake, there is a concomitant loss of calcium.

Chapter 5
Chronic Illnesses Associated with Calcium-Poor Diets

The health repercussions of avoiding milk and milk products are not limited to the increased risk of osteoporosis. While it is true that calcium is the only nutrient that's difficult to obtain without dairy (aside from vitamin D, if you avoid sun exposure), milk is unique in that it offers such a wide range of nutrients. There are many reasons that your calcium intake should be at its optimum: people with a high intake of calcium are likely to have a lower risk of obesity, hypertension, colon cancer, breast cancer, ovarian cancer, PMS and kidney stones.

Hypertension

Otherwise known as high blood pressure, this malady afflicts roughly 60 million North Americans, most of whom, if diagnosed, are put on some kind of medication to get things under control. "Wouldn't it be nice," thought some researchers, "if we could find some sort of dietary pattern that would bring blood pressure back to normal and avoid the need for drugs." Great idea! So they set about testing some popular theories. When they added eight servings of fruits and vegetables to a typical Western diet, the subjects' blood pressure dropped. When they added three servings of milk and milk products to the veggie-enhanced plan, the subjects' blood

pressure dropped again, but this time the drop was *twice as much* as when they simply increased their fruit and vegetable intake. Other research would lend support to the notion that this phenomenal effect was due to the increased calcium intake, but it's possible that it's due to the combination of minerals contained in milk, namely calcium, potassium and magnesium. The fruits and vegetables certainly added to the total intake of these minerals, but there is no other single food that contains these elements to the same degree as in milk.

But not so fast; there's another issue at stake here. The real importance of high blood pressure is that it's the major factor associated with stroke. An impressive amount of research has shown that when people are on diets very low in animal fat and protein, their risk for certain types of stroke rises considerably. Conversely, as intake of animal fat and protein rises, risk of stroke decreases. Don't take my word for it, check out the references under "Hypertension" at the end of the book. Do you suppose it's coincidental that milk and milk products are not only rich in the minerals cited, but also a good source of protein and, in the case of whole milk, fat? I think not. An interesting little side-note here is that there is an association between hypertension and osteoporosis: people with osteoporosis are also likely to have or develop hypertension, both of which are manifestations of a calcium-poor diet. Another coincidence?

In a nutshell, people who have adequate fat, protein, magnesium, potassium and calcium are less likely to suffer from hypertension and stroke.

Colon Cancer

The possible connection between diet and colon cancer has been a hot topic for quite a while now, with fiber, the most obvious potential association, being investigated first, and then vegetables and fruits. Certainly we would all benefit from a high intake of these hallowed representatives of the plant world, but whether they have a role in the prevention of colon cancer is hotly debated.

Evidence now points to what at first seemed a long shot in the colon cancer prevention sweepstakes: calcium. The most likely theory supporting a preventative role for calcium is the idea that it binds up bile salts, thereby exerting damage control in the lining of the colon. Whatever its pathway as colon protector, the published research seems to be in agreement: more calcium, less colon cancer. Several medical journals, including the *Journal of the National Cancer Institute* and *Nutrition and Cancer*, have reported studies in which people with low-calcium diets are significantly more likely to develop colon cancer than are people who consume a diet rich in calcium. These studies are not necessarily definitive, and I can't promise that those whose calcium intake is in the area of 1000 mg per day will never develop colon cancer, but the evidence is pretty persuasive.

Breast Cancer and Ovarian Cancer

The studies linking breast cancer prevention with high calcium intake are not numerous. The evidence comes mainly from the famous *Harvard Nurses' Health Study*, which found that pre-menopausal women who consumed greater amounts of calcium were less likely to get breast cancer than those with low calcium intake. The same was not found to be true of the older, post-menopausal nurses.

There is great excitement, however, about research that links a high *milk* intake with a lower risk of developing breast cancer, especially in women whose intake of milk was high when they were children. Scientists aren't quite sure why this is, but speculation has focused on a fatty acid in milk fat called conjugated linoleic acid, or CLA. This substance has been shown to be anti-carcinogenic in animal studies, as have other milk-fat ingredients such as sphingomyelin, myristic acid and butyric acid. It's also possible that the vitamin D in fortified milk plays a role. Of all the single foods studied, milk is a leading contender for breast-cancer risk reduction.

So far, the only nutrient that seems to affect a woman's risk of getting ovarian cancer is—you guessed it—calcium. Again, the reason isn't clear, but the studies are pretty persuasive: women who have an intake of calcium around the 1,000 mg mark have a decided advantage when it comes to avoiding ovarian cancer.

PMS

Premenstrual syndrome is no laughing matter, as millions of women and their families can attest. Women whose low calcium intake is replaced with a diet focusing on high-calcium foods experience a marked improvement in their fight with their hormones. It's thought to be the calcium, but it could be the combination of nutrients that are in these calcium-rich foods. It's no secret to dietitians that a high calcium intake is a marker for a generally sound, well-rounded diet. It's also no secret that there is no supplement that can mimic the nutrient profile of a nutrient-dense food.

Kidney Stones

For decades, maybe even centuries, people with kidney stones have been told to lay off dairy products because of their rich calcium content. On the surface, this made sense: kidney stones are, after all, made up mostly of calcium. But superficial solutions aren't always the best. It has now been proven that diets rich in dairy calcium actually hinder the formation of kidney stones. It's the foods that are rich in calcium *and* oxalic acid (spinach, for instance) that do the damage. Since this calcium is not absorbed, thanks to the oxalic acid, it is instead deposited in the kidneys. (Not all kidney stones are calcium oxalate, just the majority, so check with your doctor before increasing your calcium intake.)

Stay tuned as science uncovers more reasons to ensure that this extremely important mineral is at the front of your mind when you are planning your diet.

Chapter 6
Calcium and the Milk-Free Diet

There are some reasons why milk and milk products may not be a regular part of your diet. You may be allergic to milk, or you might have lactose intolerance. Perhaps you simply don't enjoy milk or dairy products, or you have a philosophy that precludes the consumption of foods of animal origin. Regardless of your reasons for not including milk products in your diet, you still need to get enough calcium. The information on supplements in Chapter 3 will help you achieve this goal, as will consumption of those non-dairy foods that are good sources of calcium. Kale and bok choy are among the best plant sources of calcium; various nuts can make a contribution, as will certain kinds of beans.

As previously discussed, there are plant foods that are relatively rich in calcium, and some that have great bioavailability of the mineral. Unfortunately, these two conditions—rich and bioavailable—hardly ever exist in the same plant. I explained this to a patient once, and her comment was, "That's just not fair." Well, fair or not, that's the way it is.

Lactose Intolerance (LI)

The most difficult topic for me to address in this book is lactose intolerance. The difficulty lies in the fact that some people are emotionally connected to this condition. One of the world's leading authorities on LI described to me the hate mail he received after publishing research showing that even people with a properly diagnosed inability to digest the natural sugar in milk can easily handle up to two glasses of milk per day—especially if they drink it along with other food. "How dare you tell me I can drink milk" was pretty much the tone of the correspondence he received.

Let me first explain what lactose is. When nutritionists discuss various sugars, they use the word "saccharides." Lactose is a disaccharide, that is, it's made up of two monosaccharides, or simple sugars: glucose and galactose. Every carbohydrate we eat that is able to be digested ends up in the small intestine as glucose, galactose or fructose, another simple sugar. Various enzymes are necessary for particular carbohydrates to be broken down to these simple sugars. In the case of lactose, the necessary enzyme is lactase (the letters "ase" tell you that something is an enzyme).

All of us (except in some extremely rare cases) produce sufficient lactase as infants to digest the lactose in our mother's milk, or in cow's milk formula if that is what the infant is being fed. In some cases, this capacity begins to diminish in early childhood, infrequently as early as weaning. In cultures that evolved without access to mammalian milk (from a cow, camel, goat or yak, for example), the body stopped producing lactase because there was no lactose for it to work on. And so we generally see continuous lactase production in people of northern European and North African descent. The elderly sometimes develop a diminished ability to produce lactase, but that might be the result of a lifetime of gradually decreasing milk intake. A temporary or secondary type of lactose intolerance can result from gastrointestinal inflammation, in which the lining of the intestines is severely irritated, affecting lactase production.

Those with lactose intolerance experience varying levels of distress, including bloating, cramps, flatulence and diarrhea. Experiencing some of these symptoms, some people decide that they have lactose intolerance and condemn themselves to a dairy-free life. Most unfortunate, both for their taste buds and especially for their bones. The approved medical test for lactose intolerance is a breath-hydrogen test, in which the amount of hydrogen in the breath is measured after the subject has been given 2 ounces (50 grams) of lactose. This is the equivalent of drinking a quart (1 liter) of milk all at once, so it's not surprising that quite a few people will be determined to be lactose intolerant.

In any event, if you suspect or have been told that you are lactose intolerant, you must come up with a plan to deal with it. As I said before, there is sound evidence that even if you have LI you can drink milk along with other foods and experience few if any problems. Otherwise, bear in mind that hard cheeses contain next to no lactose and that

the friendly bacteria in yogurt does a nice job of dispensing with the lactose found there. You can also avail yourself of milk products that have lactase added, or buy lactase tablets and take them before drinking milk or consuming milk products.

There is a huge difference between lactose intolerance and milk allergy. If you have lactose intolerance, follow the above recommendations. If you have a milk allergy, then you have to avoid milk products altogether.

Milk Allergy

Fortunately, milk allergy is very rare in adults—roughly 0.5% of the population. Approximately 3% to 5% of children will experience an allergy to milk, but the vast majority of them (95%) outgrow it by age three. The allergic reaction to milk is actually a reaction to one of the three milk proteins: lactalbumin, lactoglobulin and casein. The reaction can range from a mild runny nose or a rash to the far less common anaphylactic shock. In any case, the only solution is to avoid milk and milk products completely.

If you must avoid all dairy, get the advice of a registered dietitian to make sure you make up for the deficiencies that a milk-free diet will lead to. Since it's almost impossible to obtain adequate calcium from a dairy-less diet, supplements are strongly recommended for those with a milk allergy.

Chapter 7
The Calcium Content of Selected Foods

Calcium is not the only vital nutrient for bone health and overall body maintenance, but it is extremely important. As a result, calcium content guides are key to helping you arrive at the optimal state of calcium nourishment. The tables below tell you the calcium content of various foods.

The following code will help you identify the foods that are the best sources of calcium:

* = Source of calcium
** = Good source of calcium
*** = Excellent source of calcium

Calcium Content of Milk Products

Food	Serving size	Calcium per serving (mg)	Rating
Brie cheese	2 oz (50 g)	92	*
Buttermilk	1 cup (250 mL)	303	***
Camembert cheese	2 oz (50 g)	194	**
Cheese, firm, such as brick, cheddar, colby, Edam and Gouda	2 oz (50 g) 1" × 1" × 3" (2.5 cm × 2.5 cm × 7.5 cm)	350	***
Cottage cheese, creamed, 2%, 1%	1/2 cup (125 mL)	76	*
Feta cheese	2 oz (50 g)	255	**
Ice cream	1/2 cup (125 mL)	90	*
Ice milk	1/2 cup (125 mL)	138	*
Milk (whole, 2%, 1%, skim*)	1 cup (250 mL)	315	***
Milk, chocolate	1 cup (250 mL)	301	***
Milk powder, dry	3 tbsp (45 mL)	308	***
Mozzarella cheese	2 oz (50 g)	287	***

Calcium Content of Milk Products (cont'd)

Food	Serving size	Calcium per serving (mg)	Rating
Mozzarella cheese, partly skimmed	2 oz (50 g)	366	***
Parmesan cheese, grated	3 tbsp (45 mL)	261	**
Processed cheese slices	2 thin (42 g)	256	**
	2 regular (62 g)	384	***
Processed cheese spread	3 tbsp (45 mL)	270	**
Ricotta cheese	1/4 cup (60 mL)	135	*
Ricotta cheese, partly skimmed	1/4 cup (60 mL)	177	**
Swiss cheese	2 oz (50 g)	480	***
Yogurt drink	1 cup (250 mL)	274	***
Yogurt, frozen	1/2 cup (125 mL)	147	*
Yogurt, fruit-flavored	3/4 cup (175 g)	240	**
Yogurt, plain	3/4 cup (175 g)	296	***

* Add about 100 mg of calcium for calcium-enriched milk

Source: The Dairy Farmers of Canada's brochure "Calcium for Life: Are You on the Right Track?" Used with permission.

Calcium Content of Some Combination Foods Made with Milk Products

Food	Serving size	Calcium per serving (mg)	Rating
Baked custard	1/2 cup (125 mL)	167	**
Custard pie	1/6 of a pie	84	*
Enchilada, meat and cheese	1	228	**
Lasagna, with cheese	1 portion	193	**
Macaroni and cheese (from mix)	1 1/2 cups (375 mL)	237	**
Milkshake	10 oz (300 mL)	338	***
Pancakes, made with milk	2 medium	194	**
Pizza, with cheese	1/2 of a 12" (30 cm)	234	**
Pudding, vanilla, chocolate	1 pudding cup	126	*

The Everyday Calcium Cookbook

Calcium Content of Some Combination Foods Made with Milk Products (cont'd)

Food	Serving size	Calcium per serving (mg)	Rating
Quiche Lorraine	$^1/_6$ of pie	220	**
Rice pudding	1 pudding cup	74	*
Soups made with milk, such as cream of broccoli, chicken, mushroom, tomato	1 cup (250 mL)	184	**

Source: The Dairy Farmers of Canada's brochure "Calcium for Life: Are You on the Right Track?" Used with permission.

Calcium Content of Other Common Foods

Food	Serving size	Calcium per serving (mg)	Rating
Almonds	$^1/_2$ cup (125 mL)	(200)[1]	**
Baked beans	1 cup (250 mL)	163	**
Bok choy, cooked	$^1/_2$ cup (125 mL)	84	*
Brazil nuts	$^1/_2$ cup (125 mL)	130	*
Bread, whole wheat or white	1 slice	24	
Broccoli, cooked	$^1/_2$ cup (125 mL)	38	
Chickpeas, cooked	1 cup (250 mL)	85	*
Chili con carne	1 cup (250 mL)	(72)	*
Collards, cooked	$^1/_2$ cup (125 mL)	81	*
Dates	$^1/_4$ cup (60 mL)	14	
Figs, dried	3	81	*
Kale, cooked	$^1/_2$ cup (125 mL)	49	
Lentils, cooked	1 cup (250 mL)	40	
Nuts, mixed	$^1/_2$ cup (125 mL)	51	
Orange	1 medium	56	*
Prunes, dried, uncooked	3 medium	12	
Raisins	$^1/_4$ cup (60 mL)	21	
Red kidney beans, cooked	1 cup (250 mL)	(52)	

Calcium Content of Other Common Foods (cont'd)

Food	Serving size	Calcium per serving (mg)	Rating
Rice, white or brown, cooked	1/2 cup (125 mL)	10	
Salmon, pink, canned, with bones	1/2–213 g can	225	**
Salmon, sockeye, canned, with bones	1/2–213 g can	243	**
Sardines, canned with bones	6 medium (72 g)	275	***
Sesame seeds	1/2 cup (125 mL)	(89)	*
Soybeans, cooked	1/2 cup (125 mL)	93	*
Soy beverage	1 cup (250 mL)	10	
Soy beverage, fortified	1 cup (250 mL)	312	***
Tofu, regular, processed with calcium sulfate[2]	1/3 cup (100 g)	150	*
White beans, cooked	1 cup (250 mL)	170	**

[1.] The numbers between parentheses indicate the calcium from these foods is known to be absorbed less efficiently by the body.

[2.] The calcium content shown for tofu is an approximation, based on products available on the market. Calcium content varies greatly from one brand to another and can be quite low. Tofu processed with magnesium chloride also contains less calcium.

Source: The Dairy Farmers of Canada's brochure "Calcium for Life: Are You on the Right Track?" Used with permission.

The Everyday Calcium Cookbook

Recipes

Any of the recipes that follow can be made using fat-reduced milk or fat-reduced cheese.

Conversion Chart for Ingredients

1 cup grated cheese = $1/4$ pound or 4 oz.

4 cups grated cheese = 1 pound or 16 oz.

1 cup flour = 1/4 pound or 4 oz.

4 cups flour = 1 pound or 16 oz.

2 tbsp lemon juice = juice of 1 lemon

1 tbsp lemon zest = peel of 1 lemon

$1/2$ cup onion = 1 medium onion

1 cup onion = 2 medium onions

1 cup bell pepper = 1 large bell pepper

1 cup celery = 2 medium stalks of celery

$1/2$ lb tomatoes = 1 cup of tomatoes = 2 medium tomatoes

Breakfast and Brunch

Ham, Cheese and Asparagus Crêpes

Great Granola

Eggs Benedict with Cheese Sauce

French Toast with Cream Cheese Filling

Fruity Omelet with Maple Yogurt

Breakfast of Champions

Overnight Cheddar Bagel Casserole

Easy Cheddar Biscuits

Ham, Cheese and Asparagus Crêpes

This great dish contains four food groups—one-stop dining!
An excellent source of calcium.

Serves 9

Preheat oven to 400°F (200°C)
13-× 9-inch (3.5 L) baking dish, buttered

⅓ cup	butter, divided	75 mL
3 cups	cut-up asparagus	750 mL
2 cups	sliced brown or white mushrooms	500 mL
4	green onions, thinly sliced	4
¼ tsp	dried thyme leaves	1 mL
1 tsp	lemon juice	5 mL
	Salt and pepper	
2 cups	shredded Swiss cheese, divided	500 mL
18	crêpes (6-inch/15 cm)	18
8	thin slices cooked ham	8
3 tbsp	all-purpose flour	45 mL
1 tsp	Dijon mustard	5 mL
1½ cups	milk	375 mL
⅓ cup	dry white wine	75 mL
¼ cup	grated Parmesan cheese	50 mL

TIP: Crêpes can be prepared up to 1 day before serving. Cover and refrigerate until ready to bake. Increase baking time to 45 minutes.

1. Melt 2 tbsp (30 mL) of the butter in a large nonstick skillet over medium-high heat. Sauté asparagus, mushrooms, onions and thyme until tender, and any liquid has evaporated. Add lemon juice, then salt and pepper to taste. Stir in 1 cup (250 mL) of the Swiss cheese.

2. Line each crêpe with 1 ham slice. Divide the cheese and vegetable mixture among the crêpes, roll each up tightly and place in prepared baking dish.

3. Melt the remaining 3 tbsp (45 mL) of butter in a large saucepan. Blend in flour and mustard. Gradually stir in milk. Cook and stir over medium heat until mixture boils and thickens. Remove from heat. Add wine and ½ cup (125 mL) of the Swiss cheese; stir until melted. Salt and pepper to taste.

4. Pour sauce over crêpes and sprinkle evenly with the remaining ½ cup (125 mL) of Swiss and the Parmesan cheese. Bake uncovered in preheated oven for 30 minutes, or until hot and lightly browned.

TIP: Crêpes can be made at home or bought. If making your own, be sure the pan is hot enough before adding the batter; drops of water should dance across the pan.

Great Granola

PER SERVING	
Calories	325
Protein (g)	7.8
Carbohydrates (g)	51.5
Fat (g)	12.2
Sat	5.2
Mono	1.8
Poly	4.2

TOP 10		
1	Calcium (mg)	151
2	Potassium (mg)	737
3	Vitamin D (µg)	–
4	Magnesium (mg)	47
5	Vitamin A (RE)	71
6	B_{12} (µg)	0.36
7	Zinc (mg)	0.9
8	Thiamin (mg)	0.19
9	Riboflavin (mg)	0.28
10	Niacin (NE)	2.7

TIP: Whenever possible, use fruit that is locally grown and in season. Frozen fruit can also be used.

You needn't be a "flake" or from the granola generation to enjoy the benefits of this recipe. You don't even have to serve it only at breakfast—it makes a great dessert!

Serves 4

1 cup	granola cereal	250 mL
1/2 cup	mixed dried fruit (raisins, apricots, dates) in chunks	125 mL
1/4 cup	walnuts or almonds	50 mL
2 cups	fresh fruit (kiwi, peach, banana, grapes, etc.), in chunks	500 mL
1 cup	plain yogurt	250 mL
	Honey (optional)	

1. Combine all ingredients and serve in 4 bowls.

Eggs Benedict with Cheese Sauce

The cheese sauce removes these Benedicts from the decadent category to the nutritious. . . . Just as delightful, but with way more calcium!

Serves 2

4	eggs	4
	White vinegar	
	Salt	
2	English muffins, sliced in half	2
4	slices of cooked ham	4

Cheese Sauce

2 tbsp	butter	30 mL
2 tbsp	all-purpose flour	30 mL
1¼ cup	hot milk	300 mL
	Salt and pepper	
3 to 4 tbsp	sharp cheddar cheese, grated	45 to 60 mL

1. *Prepare Cheese Sauce:* In a small saucepan, warm butter and stir in flour. Cook over medium heat for 1 minute while stirring. Whisk in hot milk. Season to taste with salt and pepper. Simmer for 6 to 8 minutes while stirring. Stir in sharp cheddar cheese and cook for 2 to 3 minutes. Remove from heat and let cool.

2. Pour water into a skillet until it reaches halfway up the sides and add vinegar and salt. Bring to boil. Reduce heat and simmer. Break each egg into small bowl, one at a time, and gently slip into water. Cook for 3 to 4 minutes. Remove eggs with slotted spoon and set aside.

3. Toast English muffin halves. Brush lightly with Cheese Sauce. Cover each half with one ham slice and one poached egg. Sprinkle with remaining Cheese Sauce. Serve 2 eggs Benedict per person with fresh fruit.

PER SERVING	
Calories	**608**
Protein (g)	**36.5**
Carbohydrates (g)	**42.1**
Fat (g)	**31.8**
Sat	15.3
Mono	10.7
Poly	2.7

TOP 10		
1	Calcium (mg)	423
2	Potassium (mg)	659
3	Vitamin D (µg)	2.6
4	Magnesium (mg)	67
5	Vitamin A (RE)	373
6	B12 (µg)	1.7
7	Zinc (mg)	3.7
8	Thiamin (mg)	0.9
9	Riboflavin (mg)	0.98
10	Niacin (NE)	13.57

TIP: Leftover cheese can be frozen, then thawed and used in sauces like this one.

French Toast with Cream Cheese Filling

TIP: Raisin bread offers a nice change for French toast.

Quebecers definitely have a way with French toast. My daughter-in-law, Nathalie, taught me this one, and it's great. A very good source of calcium.

Serves 6

12	slices of milk bread	12
8 oz	strawberry cream cheese	250 g
6	eggs	6
3/4 cup	milk	175 mL
1 tsp	vanilla	5 mL
	Butter	
	Confectioner's (icing) sugar	
2 cups	mixed berries (blueberries, raspberries, strawberries)	500 mL
	Maple syrup	

1. Remove crust from bread (optional). Spread cream cheese evenly on half the bread slices; top with remaining slices.

2. Whip together eggs, milk and vanilla, and pour mixture into a shallow dish.

3. Dip each sandwich in egg mixture, turning it over to cover evenly.

4. Heat a bit of butter in a nonstick frying pan and fry sandwiches at medium-low heat for 2½ to 3 minutes on each side or until they are golden brown on both sides. Add butter to the frying pan as needed.

   Sprinkle with icing sugar, cut and serve with mixed berries and maple syrup.

Fruity Omelet with Maple Yogurt

We normally think of omelets as containing veggies, but thinking outside the box created this great way to add extra nutrients to this all-day breakfast dish.

Serves 4

7	large eggs	7
1 cup	fruit yogurt	250 mL
1/2 cup	table (15% or 18%) cream	125 mL
1/4 cup	maple syrup	50 mL
2 tbsp	butter	30 mL
8	seedless green grapes	8
6	fresh strawberries, hulled and halved	6
1	banana, sliced	1
	Maple syrup	

1. In a large bowl, whisk eggs for 20 to 30 seconds. Stir in yogurt, cream and maple syrup until smooth. Set aside.

2. In a large nonstick skillet, heat butter over medium heat and pour in egg mixture. Cover and cook omelet for about 8 minutes, or until preferred doneness.

3. Top with grapes, strawberries and banana and drizzle with maple syrup. Cook for another 2 minutes. Remove from heat and serve immediately.

PER SERVING	
Calories	385
Protein (g)	14.6
Carbohydrates (g)	35.4
Fat (g)	21
Sat	10.3
Mono	6.8
Poly	1.8

TOP 10		
1	Calcium (mg)	167
2	Potassium (mg)	465
3	Vitamin D (µg)	0.8
4	Magnesium (mg)	32
5	Vitamin A (RE)	253
6	B_{12} (µg)	0.97
7	Zinc (mg)	2.1
8	Thiamin (mg)	0.1
9	Riboflavin (mg)	0.53
10	Niacin (NE)	3.56

TIP: Maple "type" syrup is perfectly acceptable in this dish—not exactly the real thing, but a heck of a lot cheaper.

Breakfast of Champions

TIP: Try washed fresh spinach or romaine in place of the lettuce.

Finally, a foolproof method for poaching eggs—and I know because I've fooled around with a lot of different methods! An excellent source of calcium.

Serves 4

Preheat broiler

1 tbsp	white vinegar	15 mL
4	cold eggs	4
4	multigrain bagels, sliced in half	4
4 tsp	butter	20 mL
4	leaves Boston or chicory lettuce	4
8	orange slices, without peel	8
4 oz	cheddar cheese, in 4 thin slices	120 g
	Salt and pepper	

1. In a small saucepan, bring 3 inches (8 cm) of water to a boil. Add vinegar. Reduce heat to simmer. Break eggs into small bowl, one at a time, and carefully let slide into water. Cook eggs 3 to 5 minutes, or until egg white is cooked but yolk is still runny. Remove eggs with a slotted spoon and drain. Set aside.

2. Toast bagels and spread butter on each half. For each sandwich, put one leaf of lettuce, 2 orange slices and a poached egg on half a bagel. Top with cheddar. Broil until cheese is melted. Add salt and pepper to taste. Cover with remaining half of bagel and serve.

Overnight Cheddar Bagel Casserole

The perfect make-ahead breakfast for a crowd.... Well, I think of eight as a crowd; it's certainly enough! An excellent source of calcium.

Serves 8

13- × 9- × 2-inch (3.5 L) shallow baking dish, greased

4	plain bagels	4
2 cups	shredded cheddar cheese	500 mL
1 1/2 cups	diced ham	375 mL
1/2 cup	diced red pepper (about 1/2 medium)	125 mL
1/2 cup	diced green bell pepper (about 1/2 medium)	125 mL
1/2 cup	thinly sliced green onions (about 4 medium)	125 mL
3 tbsp	butter	45 mL
9	eggs	9
2 1/2 cups	milk	625 mL
2 tbsp	Dijon mustard	30 mL
1 tsp	salt	5 mL
4 oz	cheddar cheese, thinly sliced	120 g

PER SERVING	
Calories	484
Protein (g)	29.9
Carbohydrates (g)	28.3
Fat (g)	27.6
Sat	14.8
Mono	8.5
Poly	2

TOP 10		
1	Calcium (mg)	448
2	Potassium (mg)	415
3	Vitamin D (µg)	1.4
4	Magnesium (mg)	47
5	Vitamin A (RE)	328
6	B$_{12}$ (µg)	1.19
7	Zinc (mg)	3
8	Thiamin (mg)	0.5
9	Riboflavin (mg)	0.68
10	Niacin (NE)	9.72

1. Cut bagels in half, so that each half resembles a half moon. Turn each half moon on its side and cut into 6 thin slices. Arrange half the bagel slices along the bottom of the baking dish.

2. In a large bowl, combine cheese, ham, red and green peppers and onions; sprinkle over bagel layer.

3. Butter one side of remaining bagel slices and arrange slices, buttered side up, on top of cheese mixture.

4. In a large bowl, whisk together eggs, milk, mustard and salt; pour evenly over bagel mixture. Cover with plastic wrap and refrigerate overnight. Remove from refrigerator one hour before baking.

5. Preheat oven to 350°F (180°C). Bake uncovered in preheated oven for 1 hour, or until a knife or toothpick inserted in center comes out clean. If top is browning too quickly, cover loosely with foil.

TIP: Try a variety of bagels for this recipe. Onion and poppy seed work well.

Easy Cheddar Biscuits

PER SERVING	
Calories	119
Protein (g)	3.7
Carbohydrates (g)	13.3
Fat (g)	5.6
Sat	2.4
Mono	2.4
Poly	0.5

TOP 10		
1	Calcium (mg)	99
2	Potassium (mg)	56
3	Vitamin D (µg)	0.1
4	Magnesium (mg)	8
5	Vitamin A (RE)	27
6	B_{12} (µg)	0.07
7	Zinc (mg)	0.4
8	Thiamin (mg)	0.12
9	Riboflavin (mg)	0.13
10	Niacin (NE)	1.71

TIP: These biscuits are a great gift idea; simply pack them in festive tins.

TIP: For a real kick, Sandy sometimes adds diced jalapeno peppers—but warn your guests!

My husband, Sandy, is the biscuit-maker in our house, and he swears by this recipe.

Makes 24 biscuits

Preheat oven to 450°F (230°C)
Baking sheet

4 cups	all-purpose baking mix	1 L
1½ cups	shredded cheddar cheese	375 mL
1 cup	milk	250 mL
¾ tsp	cayenne pepper	3 mL

1. In a large bowl, combine all ingredients until dough clings together to form a ball. On a floured surface, gently knead dough and roll out to ½-inch (1 cm) thick.

2. Cut out biscuits using a cookie cutter or the rim of a glass. Brush with milk and place on baking sheet. Bake in preheated oven for about 10 minutes, or until golden.

Appetizers

Herbed Brie Cheese Balls

Pesto Bruschetta on Focaccia

Garlic Crostini with Caramelized Onions

Savory Ham and Swiss Tartlets

Cheese and Chicken Quesadillas

Chunky Nacho Cheese Dip

Cheddar Cheese Ball

Beanie Buns

Creamy Herb Dip

Herbed Brie Cheese Balls

PER SERVING	
(1 appetizer)	
Calories	303
Protein (g)	10.6
Carbohydrates (g)	34.5
Fat (g)	15
Sat	4.5
Mono	22.6
Poly	6.5

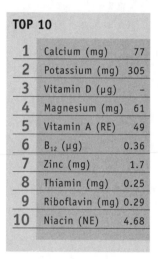

TOP 10		
1	Calcium (mg)	77
2	Potassium (mg)	305
3	Vitamin D (µg)	–
4	Magnesium (mg)	61
5	Vitamin A (RE)	49
6	B₁₂ (µg)	0.36
7	Zinc (mg)	1.7
8	Thiamin (mg)	0.25
9	Riboflavin (mg)	0.29
10	Niacin (NE)	4.68

TIP: If you're wary of the figs, Mandarin orange segments work equally well.

The figs make these cheese balls a bit exotic, but many people have never had a fresh fig. And what's an appetizer for, if not to stimulate conversation as well as appetite?

Makes 10 appetizers

1	round brie cheese	1
	Fresh herbs, chopped	
10	nut bread slices	10
10	fresh figs, sliced	10

1. Shape 1-inch (2.5 cm) cubes of brie cheese into balls, and roll in your favorite fresh herbs.
2. Top crusty nut bread slices with a fig slice and cheese ball. Garnish with fresh herbs.

Pesto Bruschetta on Focaccia

Personally, I think bottled pesto is the best thing since sliced bread—all the flavor, none of the work!

Makes 30 appetizers

Preheat barbecue to medium
2 baking sheets, lined with foil

1/4 cup	butter, melted	50 mL
1 1/2 tbsp	basil pesto	25 mL
1	rectangular loaf focaccia bread (340 g),	1
	cut into 15 slices	1
2 1/2 cups	pre-shredded Italian cheese blend	625 mL
6	plum tomatoes, sliced	6
	Chopped fresh basil	

1. Combine butter and pesto; brush on one side of each bread slice. Place bread directly on preheated grill, buttered side down. Cook, with lid open, over medium heat until lightly toasted, about 2 or 3 minutes.

2. Arrange the bread slices, toasted side up, on prepared baking sheets. Top each with 2 heaping tbsp (30 mL) of Italian cheese blend and sliced tomatoes.

3. Place each baking sheet on grill and cook, with lid closed, over medium heat until underside of bread is toasted, about 3 or 4 minutes. Cut slices in half and garnish with basil. Serve immediately.

PER SERVING	
(1 appetizer)	
Calories	79
Protein (g)	3.8
Carbohydrates (g)	6
Fat (g)	4.7
Sat	2.6
Mono	1.6
Poly	0.2

TOP 10		
1	Calcium (mg)	98
2	Potassium (mg)	58
3	Vitamin D (µg)	0.1
4	Magnesium (mg)	4
5	Vitamin A (RE)	54
6	B_{12} (µg)	0.02
7	Zinc (mg)	0.1
8	Thiamin (mg)	0.04
9	Riboflavin (mg)	0.07
10	Niacin (NE)	1.09

TIP: Mozzarella or Monterey Jack also work well in this recipe.

Garlic Crostini with Caramelized Onions

I remember the first time I saw a recipe for caramelized onions. I thought, "Brilliant! Why didn't I think of that?" Well, I didn't, but I love using them, especially in this recipe.

Makes 24 appetizers

Preheat barbecue to medium
2 baking sheets, lined with foil

¼ cup	butter, melted	50 mL
1	clove garlic, minced	1
	Salt and pepper	
24	slices (½-inch/1 cm) coarse-textured baguette	24
8 oz	mozzarella, thinly sliced	250 g
	Caramelized Onions (see recipe)	
	Hot peppers, chopped, to taste	

1. In a small bowl, combine butter and garlic; add salt and pepper to taste. Brush on one side of each bread slice.

2. Place bread directly on preheated grill, buttered side down. Cook, with lid open, over medium heat until lightly toasted, about 2 or 3 minutes.

3. Arrange the bread slices, toasted side up, on prepared baking sheets. Top each with mozzarella and about 1 tbsp (15 mL) of caramelized onions. Place each baking sheet on grill and cook, with lid closed, over medium heat until underside of bread is toasted, about 3 or 4 minutes.

4. Garnish with hot peppers. Serve immediately.

Caramelized Onions

Makes 1½ cups (375 mL)

3 tbsp	butter	45 mL
3	large onions, sliced	3
1½ tsp	sugar	7 mL
	Salt and pepper	

1. Melt butter in a large nonstick skillet. Add onions and toss to coat. Cook and stir over medium-high heat until browned, about 5 minutes.

2. Add ¼ cup (50 mL) of water and the sugar to pan, reduce heat to medium and cook, stirring occasionally, until liquid has evaporated and onions are tender and very brown, about 10 minutes. Add salt and pepper to taste.

TIP: Try Vidalia onions in this recipe—they're excellent.

Savory Ham and Swiss Tartlets

TIP: Look for frozen tart shells that don't contain hydrogenated vegetable oil or shortening.

Baby tarts are the ideal finger food: no mess, no fuss. But don't serve too many, or people will be too full to enjoy the main course!

Makes 24 appetizers

Preheat oven to 375°F (190°C)
Large baking sheet

2 cups	finely shredded Swiss cheese	500 mL
2/3 cup	finely chopped cooked ham	150 mL
1/3 cup	chopped green onions (about 3 medium)	75 mL
1/3 cup	sour cream	75 mL
	Salt and pepper	
24	frozen unbaked 3-inch (7.5 cm) tart shells	24

1. Combine Swiss cheese, ham, onions and sour cream in a medium bowl; mix well. Add salt and pepper to taste. This preparation can be refrigerated up to 2 days before using.

2. Place tart shells on baking sheet and bake in preheated oven for 10 minutes. Remove from oven. Divide cheese mixture evenly among shells. Return to oven and bake 10 minutes longer, or until filling is hot and melted.

Variation

Savory Mushroom and Oka Tartlets: Use finely shredded Canadian Oka instead of Swiss cheese, and replace ham with 1½ cups (375 mL) finely chopped mushrooms sautéed in 1 tbsp (15 mL) butter.

Cheese and Chicken Quesadillas

The recipe calls for mild salsa but, olé, let's live it up with something a little spicier! An excellent source of calcium.

Serves 4

8	large tortillas	8
1 cup	mild Mexican salsa	250 mL
2 cups	cooked chicken, cut in pieces	500 mL
2 cups	grated mild cheddar or Monterey Jack cheese	500 mL
	Vegetable oil	
	Sour cream (optional)	
	Guacamole (optional)	

1. For each quesadilla, place one tortilla on a large plate. Spread with salsa and arrange chicken pieces evenly over salsa. Sprinkle with cheese and cover with another tortilla.

2. Heat some vegetable oil in a large skillet. When hot, slide quesadilla into skillet. Cook each quesadilla over medium heat for 4 to 5 minutes. Gently turn quesadilla and cook for an additional 3 to 4 minutes. Quesadillas can also be cooked on a buttered barbecue grill.

3. Place each cooked quesadilla on a plate and cut into 4 wedges. Top with sour cream and guacamole, if using.

4. Serve quesadillas hot or cold. They will keep for 2 to 3 days in the refrigerator. Reheat in an oven preheated to 350°F (180°C) for 5 to 10 minutes.

PER SERVING	
(1 appetizer)	
Calories	747
Protein (g)	45
Carbohydrates (g)	67.8
Fat (g)	32.1
Sat	15.4
Mono	11.5
Poly	3

TOP 10		
1	Calcium (mg)	482
2	Potassium (mg)	513
3	Vitamin D (µg)	0.2
4	Magnesium (mg)	71
5	Vitamin A (RE)	205
6	B_{12} (µg)	0.7
7	Zinc (mg)	4.2
8	Thiamin (mg)	0.69
9	Riboflavin (mg)	0.69
10	Niacin (NE)	20.14

TIP: Cooked beef or pork strips can replace the chicken.

Chunky Nacho Cheese Dip

TIP: To cut down on the calories (and trans fats), make your own chips by baking pita triangles in a 300°F (150°C) oven for 10 minutes. You can also serve raw veggies for dipping.

This is a really popular dip—why should it be served only in pubs or Mexican restaurants?

Makes 2½ cups (625 mL)

2 tbsp	butter	30 mL
1	medium onion, chopped	1
1 cup	finely chopped tomatoes	250 mL
1½ tbsp	all-purpose flour	25 mL
1 cup	milk	250 mL
1½ cups	shredded cheddar cheese	375 mL
2 tbsp	chopped jalapeno chili peppers or small hot peppers	30 mL
	Hot pepper sauce or chili powder	
	Tortilla chips	

1. In a medium nonstick skillet, melt butter. Add onion and tomatoes; sauté over medium heat until onion is tender.

2. In a small bowl, gradually stir milk into flour until smooth. Add to pan. Cook and stir over low heat until mixture boils and thickens.

3. Remove from heat; add cheddar cheese and stir until cheese is melted.

4. Stir in chilies; add hot pepper sauce or chili powder to taste.

5. Serve hot with tortilla chips for dipping.

Cheddar Cheese Ball

This is one of those old-fashioned recipes that I almost didn't include just because it is so old hat. But just three servings give you as much calcium as a glass of milk—and it's great with a glass of wine!

Makes 2 cups (500 mL)

12	slices bacon	12
3 cups	shredded cheddar cheese	750 mL
1	package (4 oz/125 g) cream cheese, softened	1
1/2 cup	chopped walnuts	125 mL
1/4 cup	chopped parsley	50 mL

1. Cook bacon until crisp; drain well, reserving 2 tbsp (30 mL) drippings. Chop bacon very finely.
2. In a large bowl, beat together cheddar and cream cheese.
3. Add reserved bacon drippings. Stir in cooked bacon bits.
4. Shape into a ball; roll in chopped nuts and parsley.
5. Wrap in plastic wrap and chill several hours or overnight to blend flavors. Let stand at room temperature for 1 hour before serving.

PER SERVING	
(4 tsp/20 mL)	
Calories	117
Protein (g)	5.4
Carbohydrates (g)	0.7
Fat (g)	10.5
Sat	5.1
Mono	3.1
Poly	1.7

TOP 10		
1	Calcium (mg)	111
2	Potassium (mg)	53
3	Vitamin D (µg)	–
4	Magnesium (mg)	10
5	Vitamin A (RE)	63
6	B_{12} (µg)	0.2
7	Zinc (mg)	0.7
8	Thiamin (mg)	0.04
9	Riboflavin (mg)	0.08
10	Niacin (NE)	1.39

TIP: Try making this with Quark instead of cream cheese for more calcium and fewer calories. You can find Quark in the dairy case at your grocery store.

Beanie Buns

PER SERVING	
(1 appetizer)	
Calories	561
Protein (g)	30.2
Carbohydrates (g)	54.2
Fat (g)	25.1
Sat	11.8
Mono	8.5
Poly	2.5

TOP 10		
1	Calcium (mg)	390
2	Potassium (mg)	630
3	Vitamin D (µg)	–
4	Magnesium (mg)	71
5	Vitamin A (RE)	130
6	B_{12} (µg)	1.41
7	Zinc (mg)	5.6
8	Thiamin (mg)	0.41
9	Riboflavin (mg)	0.49
10	Niacin (NE)	11.6

TIP: Lean ground pork, chicken or turkey may be substituted for beef. Hot dog buns work as well as hamburger buns.

You don't need to be a cowboy to enjoy this combination of beef and beans. . . . Yahoo! An excellent source of calcium

Serves 4

Preheat broiler

1/2 lb	lean ground beef	250 g
1	can (14 oz/398 mL) beans with pork	1
1/4 cup	bottled barbecue sauce	50 mL
4	hamburger buns	4
11/4 cups	shredded Colby cheese, divided	300 mL

1. In a large nonstick skillet, cook meat over medium heat and drain.

2. Add beans and barbecue sauce; bring to a boil over medium-high heat. Reduce heat and simmer, uncovered, for 5 minutes or until heated through.

3. Split buns and toast under broiler.

4. Sprinkle 1/4 cup (50 mL) of the Colby cheese on each half bun and broil until cheese is melted.

5. Spoon equal amounts of hot bean mixture onto each half bun. Top with remaining 1 cup (250 mL) Colby cheese. Broil until cheese is melted and serve.

Creamy Herb Dip

Bear in mind that using yogurt will give you more calcium. For the best of both worlds (calcium plus sour cream's great flavor), I often use half yogurt, half sour cream.

Makes about 1²/₃ cups (400 mL)

1	package (4 oz/125 g) cream cheese, softened	1
³/₄ cup	plain yogurt or sour cream	175 mL
1 tbsp	finely chopped green onion	15 mL
1 tbsp	finely chopped fresh parsley	15 mL
1 tsp	dried dillweed	5 mL
	Seasoned salt	

1. In a medium bowl, beat cream cheese until smooth; gradually beat in yogurt. Stir in onion, parsley and dill. Add seasoned salt to taste.

2. Chill at least 1 hour to blend flavors. Serve with assorted crisp vegetables or crackers for dipping.

Variation

"Some-Like-It-Hot" Dip: Omit parsley and dillweed. Add 1 tsp (5 mL) prepared horseradish, ³/₄ tsp (3 mL) Worcestershire sauce and ¹/₄ tsp (1 mL) hot pepper sauce. Stir in 1 cup (250 mL) drained, flaked crabmeat or finely chopped cooked shrimp. Makes about 2 cups (500 mL).

PER SERVING	
(4 tsp/20 mL)	
Calories	29
Protein (g)	0.9
Carbohydrates (g)	0.8
Fat (g)	2.4
Sat	1.5
Mono	0.7
Poly	0.1

TOP 10

1	Calcium (mg)	21
2	Potassium (mg)	32
3	Vitamin D (µg)	–
4	Magnesium (mg)	2
5	Vitamin A (RE)	27
6	B₁₂ (µg)	0.8
7	Zinc (mg)	0.1
8	Thiamin (mg)	0.01
9	Riboflavin (mg)	0.03
10	Niacin (NE)	0.13

Soups

Atlantic Salmon Chowder

Sweet Seafood Soup

Cheddary Cauliflower Soup

Creamy French Onion Soup

Gouda and Vegetable Chowder

Tomato Soup

Cream of Mushroom and Almond Soup

Corn Chowder

Atlantic Salmon Chowder

TIP: If you have leftover cooked salmon, it works very well in this chowder. You can also use fresh salmon and cook it in the chowder.

My sons call me the Soup Queen—a moniker I wear with pride. Soups are my specialty because they're so easy and forgiving. Almost anything goes. This one reflects my Nova Scotia background.

Serves 6

1 tbsp	butter	15 mL
1/2 cup	chopped onions (about 1/2 medium)	125 mL
1/2 cup	chopped celery (about 2 medium ribs)	125 mL
1/4 cup	chopped green bell pepper (about 1/4 medium)	50 mL
1	garlic clove, finely chopped	1
3 cups	diced potatoes (about 3 medium)	750 mL
1 cup	diced carrots (about 2 medium)	250 mL
1 cup	chicken broth	250 mL
1/2 tsp	dill seeds	2 mL
1 cup	diced zucchini (about 1 medium)	250 mL
1 1/2 cup	milk	375 mL
1	can (10 oz/284 mL) cream-style corn	1
1	can (7.5 oz/212 mL) salmon, drained	1
	Pepper	
1/2 cup	chopped fresh parsley	125 mL
	French baguette bread	

1. In a large saucepan melt butter; sauté onions, celery, green pepper and garlic for 5 minutes while stirring.

2. Stir in potatoes, carrots, broth, 1 cup (250 mL) water and dill. Bring to boil. Reduce heat, cover and simmer for 20 minutes.

3. Add zucchini and cook for another 5 minutes.

4. Stir in milk, corn and salmon; season to taste with pepper. Cook over low heat for 5 to 10 minutes.

5. Sprinkle with fresh parsley before serving. Serve with French baguette bread.

Sweet Seafood Soup

The sweet potato in this soup is a surprise and a great contributor of beta carotene. This really is a meal in a bowl.

Serves 4

2 tbsp	olive oil	30 mL
2	garlic cloves, finely chopped	2
2	sweet potatoes, peeled and diced	2
1	red onion, chopped	1
3 cups	vegetable broth	750 mL
1	can (14 oz/284 mL) clams, drained	1
8 oz	large scallops, sliced	250 g
8 oz	large shrimp, shelled, deveined and cut in half	250 g
1¼ cup	milk	300 mL
½ cup	table (15% or 18%) cream	125 mL
2	egg yolks	2
	Salt and pepper	
	Savory	
	Thyme	
	Fresh chives	

1. In a large saucepan, sauté garlic, sweet potatoes and onion in oil, stirring constantly.

2. Stir in broth and bring to boil. Reduce heat, cover and simmer for 15 minutes.

3. Add clams, scallops and shrimp; mix well. Stir in milk and cream. Simmer over medium-low heat for 7 minutes. Remove from heat and let stand for 3 minutes.

4. Stir in egg yolks and season to taste with salt, pepper, savory and thyme. Mix well.

5. Serve immediately, garnished with fresh chives.

PER SERVING	
Calories	456
Protein (g)	35.5
Carbohydrates (g)	35.1
Fat (g)	19.1
Sat	6.3
Mono	8.3
Poly	2

TOP 10		
1	Calcium (mg)	244
2	Potassium (mg)	973
3	Vitamin D (µg)	2.6
4	Magnesium (mg)	86
5	Vitamin A (RE)	1325
6	B_{12} (µg)	39.46
7	Zinc (mg)	3.1
8	Thiamin (mg)	0.19
9	Riboflavin (mg)	0.53
10	Niacin (NE)	10.54

TIP: You can substitute canned oysters for the clams in this recipe.

Cheddary Cauliflower Soup

PER SERVING	
Calories	576
Protein (g)	34.2
Carbohydrates (g)	26.3
Fat (g)	37.9
Sat	23
Mono	10.8
Poly	1.8

TOP 10

1	Calcium (mg)	775
2	Potassium (mg)	853
3	Vitamin D (µg)	2.2
4	Magnesium (mg)	65
5	Vitamin A (RE)	385
6	B₁₂ (µg)	1.1
7	Zinc (mg)	3.6
8	Thiamin (mg)	0.21
9	Riboflavin (mg)	0.76
10	Niacin (NE)	11.98

TIP: Serve this soup with a dark rye or pumpernickel bread—a great combination!

I'm certainly not the first person to suggest that hot soup on a cold day is a great idea. It warms the cockles of your heart!

Serves 4

3 tbsp	butter	45 mL
2/3 cup	chopped onion (about 1 medium)	150 mL
5 cups	coarsely chopped cauliflower	1.25 L
2	cans (each 10 oz/284 mL) chicken broth	2
1/3 cup	all-purpose flour	75 mL
3 cups	milk	750 mL
2 1/2 cups	shredded cheddar cheese	625 mL
1/4 cup	chopped fresh parsley	50 mL
	Salt and pepper	

1. In a large saucepan, melt butter. Sauté onion until tender.

2. Stir in cauliflower and chicken broth. Bring to a boil over medium-high heat. Reduce heat, cover and simmer for 12 minutes, or until cauliflower is tender.

3. In a large bowl, gradually stir milk into flour until smooth. Add to saucepan. Cook and stir over medium heat until mixture boils and thickens.

4. Remove from heat, add cheese and parsley and stir until cheese is melted. Add salt and pepper to taste.

Creamy French Onion Soup

I should probably call this Swiss onion soup, since it's the Swiss cheese that gives it an edge, but some names are sacred. Still, a rose by any other name... An excellent source of calcium.

Serves 4

Preheat broiler
4 ovenproof soup bowls

¼ cup	butter	50 mL
3 cups	thinly sliced onions (about 3 medium)	750 mL
5 tsp	chicken broth mix	25 mL
¼ cup	all-purpose flour	50 mL
1¾ cups	milk	450 mL
¾ cup	shredded mozzarella cheese	175 mL
¾ cup	shredded Swiss cheese	175 mL
	Salt and pepper	
	Croutons	

1. Melt butter in a large saucepan; cook and stir onions over medium heat for about 10 minutes, or until softened.

2. Stir in 1½ cups (375 mL) water and broth mix. Bring to boil. Cover and simmer for 15 minutes.

3. In a medium bowl, gradually stir milk into flour until smooth. Add to saucepan. Cook and stir over medium heat until mixture boils and thickens. Remove from heat.

4. Toss together mozzarella and Swiss cheeses. Add ¾ cup (175 mL) of the cheese mixture to the soup; stir until melted. Add salt and pepper to taste.

5. Ladle into 4 ovenproof soup bowls; sprinkle with croutons. Top with remaining cheese. Broil until cheese is melted. Serve.

PER SERVING	
Calories	380
Protein (g)	17.2
Carbohydrates (g)	20.9
Fat (g)	25.7
Sat	15.7
Mono	7.3
Poly	1.2

TOP 10		
1	Calcium (mg)	490
2	Potassium (mg)	358
3	Vitamin D (µg)	1.5
4	Magnesium (mg)	41
5	Vitamin A (RE)	280
6	B_{12} (µg)	0.66
7	Zinc (mg)	2
8	Thiamin (mg)	0.13
9	Riboflavin (mg)	0.39
10	Niacin (NE)	4.79

TIP: Emmenthal cheese tastes great in onion soup.

Gouda and Vegetable Chowder

PER SERVING	
Calories	292
Protein (g)	19.2
Carbohydrates (g)	15.7
Fat (g)	17.4
Sat	10.5
Mono	5
Poly	0.8

TOP 10		
1	Calcium (mg)	403
2	Potassium (mg)	546
3	Vitamin D (µg)	0.9
4	Magnesium (mg)	39
5	Vitamin A (RE)	598
6	B$_{12}$ (µg)	0.88
7	Zinc (mg)	2.3
8	Thiamin (mg)	0.12
9	Riboflavin (mg)	0.4
10	Niacin (NE)	7.23

TIP: Serve this soup with a whole-grain bread, and have some fruit for dessert—what a winning combination!

The two food groups that are the most neglected by North Americans are the vegetable and fruit group and the milk products group. This recipe addresses both problems. An excellent source of calcium.

Serves 6

2 tbsp	butter	30 mL
1	medium onion, chopped	1
2 cups	chopped cauliflower	500 mL
2 cups	chopped broccoli	500 mL
1 cup	grated carrot (about 2 medium)	250 mL
2	cans (each 10 oz/284 mL) condensed chicken broth	2
1/4 cup	all-purpose flour	50 mL
2 cups	milk	500 mL
2 cups	shredded Gouda cheese, divided	375 mL
	Salt and pepper	
	Croutons	

1. Melt butter in a large saucepan. Cook and stir onion over medium-high heat until tender.

2. Add cauliflower, broccoli, carrot and condensed chicken broth. Bring to boil. Reduce heat, cover and simmer for 10 minutes, or until vegetables are tender.

3. In a medium bowl, whisk milk into flour until smoothly combined; add to saucepan. Cook and stir over medium heat until mixture boils and thickens. Remove pan from heat.

4. Add 1½ cups (375 mL) of the Gouda cheese and stir until cheese is melted. Season with salt and pepper.

5. To serve, sprinkle with the remaining ½ cup (125 mL) of cheese and add croutons.

Tomato Soup

Not to take anything away from canned soups—they have their place in our busy world—but this soup is so easy and satisfying, it's a shame to go for canned! An excellent source of calcium.

Serves 2

10	red tomatoes	10
1 tbsp	olive oil	15 mL
1	onion, minced	1
Pinch	sugar	Pinch
2	sprigs fresh basil, chopped	2
1	sprig fresh oregano, whole	1
1 tbsp	salt	15 mL
2 tsp	pepper	10 mL
1/4 cup	butter	60 mL
1/4 cup	all-purpose flour	60 mL
3 cups	warm milk	500 mL

1. Scald tomatoes so they peel easily and chop them.

2. Heat olive oil in a fry pan and sauté onion. Add tomatoes and sugar, and bring to a boil. Add basil, oregano, salt and pepper, and simmer until tomatoes are mushy, then remove oregano.

3. While tomatoes are cooking, melt butter in a large saucepot. Blend in flour and gradually add milk. Bring to a boil and stir until thickened.

4. Gradually add tomatoes with a ladle, stirring constantly. Simmer, stirring often, then enjoy! Soup may be served as is or blended into a delicious cream of tomato soup.

PER SERVING	
Calories	582
Protein (g)	17.4
Carbohydrates (g)	47.9
Fat (g)	37.7
Sat	19.7
Mono	13.6
Poly	2

TOP 10		
1	Calcium (mg)	500
2	Potassium (mg)	1281
3	Vitamin D (µg)	4.1
4	Magnesium (mg)	96
5	Vitamin A (RE)	697
6	B_{12} (µg)	0.42
7	Zinc (mg)	2
8	Thiamin (mg)	0.39
9	Riboflavin (mg)	0.83
10	Niacin (NE)	6.67

TIP: Try Roma tomatoes for this soup; they're usually less expensive, and they're just as tasty.

Cream of Mushroom and Almond Soup

PER SERVING	
Calories	401
Protein (g)	7.4
Carbohydrates (g)	11.6
Fat (g)	37.3
Sat	21
Mono	12.2
Poly	2.2

TOP 10		
1	Calcium (mg)	155
2	Potassium (mg)	368
3	Vitamin D (µg)	0.7
4	Magnesium (mg)	42
5	Vitamin A (RE)	323
6	B_{12} (µg)	0.2
7	Zinc (mg)	0.8
8	Thiamin (mg)	0.07
9	Riboflavin (mg)	0.31
10	Niacin (NE)	3.57

TIP: Sprinkle some toasted slivered almonds on top of the soup for added calcium and crunch.

The almonds in this soup contribute to both the calcium content and the taste. This is definitely not your Granny's mushroom soup.

Serves 4

2 tbsp	butter	30 mL
1	medium onion, finely chopped	1
1¼ cup	sliced white mushrooms, divided	300 mL
¼ cup	minced almonds	50 mL
1 cup	milk	250 mL
2 cups	beef broth	500 mL
1 tbsp	corn starch, diluted in 3 tbsp of water	15 mL
1¼ cup	35% cream	300 mL
	Salt and pepper	
	Thyme	

1. In a large saucepan melt butter; sauté onion, ½ cup (125 mL) of the mushrooms and the almonds for 5 minutes, or until almonds are golden.

2. Stir in milk. Purée in food processor or blender and return to saucepan.

3. Stir in beef broth. Add remaining mushrooms and stir in diluted cornstarch. Bring to boil, stirring constantly. Reduce to low heat.

4. Stir in cream and season to taste with salt, pepper and thyme. Heat through for 2 to 3 minutes, stirring constantly. Serve immediately.

The Everyday Calcium Cookbook

Corn Chowder

Serves 4

3	vegetable broth cubes	3
1/4 cup	butter	50 mL
1/2 cup	finely chopped onion (about 1/2 medium)	125 mL
1/2 cup	finely chopped celery (about 2 medium ribs)	125 mL
1/4 cup	all-purpose flour	50 mL
2 cups	milk	500 mL
1/2 cup	light cream	125 mL
3 cups	frozen corn	750 mL
1 1/2 cups	shredded, peeled potatoes (about 1/2 lb)	375 mL
1 tsp	dried basil	5 mL
	Salt and pepper	

1. Add vegetable broth to 2 cups (500 mL) boiling water and set aside.

2. Melt butter in a large saucepan, add onion and celery and sauté until onion is transparent. Add flour and stir until well mixed. Continue stirring over low heat until mixture starts to turn brown. Add broth slowly, stirring constantly. Increase heat and bring to a boil.

3. Warm milk and cream in microwave, then add to soup mixture, along with shredded corn, potato, basil and salt and pepper to taste. Simmer for 20 to 25 minutes, stirring often.

4. Adjust seasoning. For best flavor, make this soup a day or two in advance and refrigerate until serving.

PER SERVING	
Calories	**398**
Protein (g)	**10.6**
Carbohydrates (g)	**48.5**
Fat (g)	**20.1**
Sat	12.1
Mono	5.6
Poly	1

TOP 10

1	Calcium (mg)	202
2	Potassium (mg)	632
3	Vitamin D (µg)	1.5
4	Magnesium (mg)	56
5	Vitamin A (RE)	239
6	B$_{12}$ (µg)	0.17
7	Zinc (mg)	1.2
8	Thiamin (mg)	0.24
9	Riboflavin (mg)	0.39
10	Niacin (NE)	4.95

TIP: For more flavor, add one whole chili pepper to the bouillon mixture at the start of the recipe and remove just prior to serving. It will add some zing without much heat.

Salads

Havarti Apple Toss

Fabulous Feta Salad

Avocado Chicken Salad

Cheddar and Garden Couscous Salad

Grilled Chicken and Swiss Cheese Salad with Curried Yogurt Dressing

High-Performance Pasta Salad

Honeyed Yogurt Fruit Salad

Picnic Potato Salad

Kitchen Sink Salad

Havarti Apple Toss

PER SERVING

Calories	506
Protein (g)	13.6
Carbohydrates (g)	44.8
Fat (g)	33.9
Sat	15.3
Mono	8.4
Poly	8.4

TOP 10

1	Calcium (mg)	358
2	Potassium (mg)	422
3	Vitamin D (µg)	–
4	Magnesium (mg)	41
5	Vitamin A (RE)	245
6	B$_{12}$ (µg)	0.17
7	Zinc (mg)	0.9
8	Thiamin (mg)	0.13
9	Riboflavin (mg)	0.29
10	Niacin (NE)	2.06

TIP: For a truly Canadian experience, use maple syrup in place of the honey.

I probably shouldn't admit this, being a nutritionist, but I'm not drawn to apples—until they're in a salad, then I love them! I think those guys at the Waldorf Hotel had the right idea when they designed the first apple salad. An excellent source of calcium.

Serves 4

1 cup	sour cream	250 mL
1/4 cup	liquid honey	50 mL
2 tsp	lemon juice	10 mL
4 cups	diced, cored red apples (about 4 medium)	1 L
1 1/4 cups	diced havarti cheese	300 mL
1 cup	sliced celery (about 4 medium ribs)	250 mL
1/2 cup	crushed walnuts	125 mL
	Leaf lettuce	

1. In a small bowl, combine sour cream, honey and lemon juice. Chill dressing at least 1 hour to blend flavors.

2. Just before serving, combine apples, havarti cheese, celery and walnuts in a large bowl.

3. Pour in dressing and toss lightly to combine. Spoon into a lettuce-lined bowl and serve.

Fabulous Feta Salad

This is the real meal deal: beans, cheese and veggies. Serve with a whole-grain pita bread and you're practically in Athens!

Serves 4

2 tbsp	olive oil	30 mL
1 tbsp	lemon juice or wine vinegar	15 mL
1/2 tsp	dried oregano	2 mL
1 cup	canned red kidney beans, rinsed and drained	250 mL
1 cup	diced tomatoes (about 2 medium)	250 mL
1 cup	diced green bell pepper (about 1 medium)	250 mL
1 cup	diced feta cheese	250 mL
1/4 cup	chopped onion (about 1/2 medium)	60 mL

1. Combine olive oil, lemon juice and oregano. Pour over other ingredients. Toss and season to taste.

PER SERVING	
Calories	209
Protein (g)	7.9
Carbohydrates (g)	14.8
Fat (g)	13.8
Sat	5.6
Mono	6.5
Poly	1

TOP 10		
1	Calcium (mg)	172
2	Potassium (mg)	318
3	Vitamin D (µg)	–
4	Magnesium (mg)	28
5	Vitamin A (RE)	92
6	B_{12} (µg)	0.52
7	Zinc (mg)	1.2
8	Thiamin (mg)	0.15
9	Riboflavin (mg)	0.34
10	Niacin (NE)	2.64

TIP: Make sure your olive oil is kept in a cool, dark place to preserve freshness. It should not be on the kitchen counter in a transparent bottle.

Avocado Chicken Salad

TIP: You could use a lime instead of the lemon. In either case, the juice helps keep the avocado from turning brown.

Avocados get a bad rap that they just don't deserve. Sure they contain more fat than other fruits (vegetables, too, for that matter), but they're packed with nutrients and well warrant a place at the table.

Serves 4

	Choice of lettuce, shredded	
1 lb	cooked chicken, diced	500 g
2/3 cup	peeled and diced avocado (about 1/2 medium)	150 mL
	Juice of 1/2 lemon	
1/2 cup	chopped red bell pepper (about 1/2 medium)	125 mL
1/2	lemon, thinly sliced	1/2
	Crusty bread	

Creamy Chive Dressing

1/2	red onion, sliced	1/2
1 cup	plain yogurt	250 mL
2/3 cup	mayonnaise	150 mL
3 tbsp	chopped chives	45 mL
2 tbsp	chopped fresh tarragon	30 mL
2 tbsp	choice of flavored vinegar	30 mL
Pinch	sugar	Pinch
	Pepper	

1. *Prepare Creamy Chive Dressing:* Place onion, yogurt, mayonnaise, chives, tarragon and vinegar in food processor and purée until smooth. Add pinch of sugar and season to taste with pepper. Mix well. Transfer into a bowl and refrigerate for 1 hour before serving.

2. Line bottoms of 4 salad plates generously with lettuce. Fill with chicken and avocado. Sprinkle with lemon juice and top with Creamy Chive Dressing. Garnish with red pepper and lemon slices. Serve cold with crusty bread.

Cheddar and Garden Couscous Salad

One of the original convenience or "instant" foods, couscous refers both to the product made from the flour of durum wheat and to the national dish of many North African countries. Use it in place of potatoes, pasta or rice.

Serves 6 as a main course

1¼ cups	chicken broth	300 mL
1 cup	instant couscous	250 mL
1½ cups	diced cheddar cheese (about 6 oz/175 g)	375 mL
1¼ cups	diced, unpeeled English cucumber (about 1 medium)	300 mL
1 cup	diced seeded tomatoes (about 2 medium)	250 mL
¾ cup	diced green bell pepper (about 1 medium)	175 mL
¼ cup	chopped green onions (about 2 medium)	50 mL
¼ cup	chopped fresh parsley or dill	50 mL
	Salt and pepper	

Dressing

⅓ cup	white wine vinegar or lemon juice	75 mL
⅓ cup	olive oil	75 mL
1	large clove garlic, minced	1
Pinch	sugar (or to taste)	Pinch

PER SERVING	
Calories	**362**
Protein (g)	**12.8**
Carbohydrates (g)	**29.1**
Fat (g)	**22**
Sat	7.7
Mono	11.6
Poly	1.5

TOP 10		
1	Calcium (mg)	230
2	Potassium (mg)	306
3	Vitamin D (µg)	0.1
4	Magnesium (mg)	30
5	Vitamin A (RE)	128
6	B_{12} (µg)	0.29
7	Zinc (mg)	1.4
8	Thiamin (mg)	0.12
9	Riboflavin (mg)	0.18
10	Niacin (NE)	4.78

1. Heat broth to boiling in a medium saucepan. Stir in couscous, cover and remove from heat. Let stand for 5 minutes. Transfer to large bowl, fluff with a fork and let cool for 10 minutes.

2. *Prepare dressing:* Combine vinegar, olive oil, garlic and sugar in a small bowl. Whisk together thoroughly.

3. Add cheddar, cucumber, tomatoes, green pepper, onions and parsley to couscous. Pour dressing over salad and toss well to coat. Add salt and pepper to taste.

TIP: This is a great main course on a warm summer day.

Grilled Chicken and Swiss Cheese Salad with Curried Yogurt Dressing

TIP: This works well with a variety of chutneys.

My daughter-in-law, Christine, introduced me to this salad; sometimes she uses broiled beef strips in place of chicken. Delicious either way, and more iron if you use the beef. An excellent source of calcium.

Serves 4

Preheat barbecue to medium

8 oz	boneless, skinless chicken breasts	250 g
1	package mixed salad greens or 1 head of romaine lettuce, washed	1
2 cups	cherry tomato halves	500 mL
1¼ cups	thinly sliced English cucumber (about 1 medium)	300 mL
8 oz	Swiss cheese, cut into matchsticks	250 g
½ cup	carrots, cut into matchsticks (about 1 medium)	125 mL
	Salt and pepper	

Curried Yogurt Dressing

1 cup	plain yogurt	250 mL
¼ cup	half-and-half (10%) cream	50 mL
2 tbsp	smooth mango chutney (or to taste)	30 mL
2 tbsp	finely chopped green onions (about 1 medium)	30 mL
1 tsp	curry powder (or to taste)	5 mL

1. *Prepare Curried Yogurt Dressing:* Combine yogurt, cream, chutney, onions and curry powder in a medium bowl. Stir until well mixed.

2. Remove 2 tbsp (30 mL) of the curried yogurt dressing and set remainder aside. Brush chicken with dressing and place on preheated grill. Cook with lid closed over medium heat for 10 minutes, or until chicken is no longer pink in center, turning once halfway through. Remove from heat and slice thinly.

3. Combine chicken, salad greens, tomatoes, cucumber, Swiss cheese and carrots in a large salad bowl. Pour remaining curried yogurt dressing over salad and toss well to coat. Add salt and pepper to taste.

High-Performance Pasta Salad

While pasta might not make an Olympic athlete out of you, it provides a satisfying meal, and the use of fruit and nuts makes this pasta salad a bit unusual. An excellent source of calcium.

Serves 6

1	package (12 oz/375 g) rotini	1
³/₄ cup	Swiss cheese, diced (about 7 oz/200 g)	175 mL
¹/₂ cup	chopped dried apricots	125 mL
¹/₂ cup	chopped dates	125 mL
¹/₂ cup	sliced almonds	125 mL
1	unpeeled apple, cubed	1
	Fresh mint to garnish (optional)	

Vinaigrette

1 tsp	orange zest	5 mL
¹/₃ cup	orange juice	75 mL
¹/₃ cup	olive oil	75 mL
¹/₄ cup	rice wine vinegar	50 mL
1 tbsp	liquid honey	15 mL

1. In a medium saucepan, cook rotini according to package directions. Drain and rinse under cold water. Refrigerate for about 10 minutes.

2. *Meanwhile, prepare the vinaigrette:* In a medium bowl, whisk together orange zest, orange juice, olive oil, rice wine vinegar and honey.

3. Combine rotini, Swiss cheese, apricots, dates, almonds and apple. Add vinaigrette and mix well. Serve garnished with fresh mint, if desired.

PER SERVING	
Calories	591
Protein (g)	19.3
Carbohydrates (g)	71.6
Fat (g)	26.7
Sat	8
Mono	14.2
Poly	2.8

TOP 10		
1	Calcium (mg)	362
2	Potassium (mg)	465
3	Vitamin D (µg)	0.4
4	Magnesium (mg)	78
5	Vitamin A (RE)	172
6	B₁₂ (µg)	0.55
7	Zinc (mg)	2.5
8	Thiamin (mg)	0.29
9	Riboflavin (mg)	0.26
10	Niacin (NE)	6.01

TIP: Give whole-grain rotini a try. It adds a nice, nutty flavor.

Honeyed Yogurt Fruit Salad

TIP: Yogurt and Honey Sauce is best when prepared in advance.

TIP: You can replace the honey with maple syrup.

To my way of thinking, this is a perfect dessert, especially in the summertime.

Serves 4

Yogurt and Honey Sauce

1 cup	plain yogurt	250 mL
3 tbsp	liquid honey	45 mL
1 tbsp	lemon juice	15 mL
1 tbsp	orange juice	15 mL
1/4 tsp	vanilla	1 mL

Fruit Salad

2	bananas, peeled and sliced	2
2	kiwis, peeled and sliced	2
1 cup	choice of seedless grapes	250 mL
1 cup	choice of peeled melon cubes	250 mL
1 cup	fresh strawberries or raspberries	250 mL

1. *Prepare Yogurt and Honey Sauce:* In a small bowl, mix all ingredients. Chill for 1 to 2 hours before serving.

2. *Prepare Fruit Salad:* Gently combine all ingredients in a large bowl. Divide among 4 dessert bowls and drizzle with Yogurt and Honey Sauce.

3. Serve immediately with preferred cookies.

Picnic Potato Salad

I think there's a rule somewhere that you can't have a picnic without potato salad. At least, that's what my husband tells me, and he makes the best ones.

Serves 8

6 cups	peeled, diced, cooked potatoes (about 1.5 lb)	1.5 L
1/3 cup	vinegar or lemon juice	75 mL
1/3 cup	chopped green onions (about 3 medium)	75 mL
1/4 cup	melted butter	50 mL
1 tbsp	chopped fresh dill, or to taste	15 mL
1 tsp	sugar	5 mL
1 1/2 cups	sliced celery (about 6 medium ribs)	375 mL
1 1/4 cups	sour cream	300 mL
3/4 cup	chopped orange or red bell pepper (about 1 medium)	175 mL
	Salt and pepper	

1. In a large, microwave-safe bowl, combine potatoes, vinegar, onions, butter, dill and sugar; toss well.

2. Microwave at high (100%) for 2 minutes, or until warm. Cover and let stand for 1 hour to blend flavors.

3. Just before serving, stir in celery, sour cream and chopped pepper. Add salt and pepper to taste.

PER SERVING	
Calories	219
Protein (g)	3.7
Carbohydrates (g)	28.1
Fat (g)	11
Sat	6.8
Mono	3.1
Poly	0.5

TOP 10		
1	Calcium (mg)	59
2	Potassium (mg)	596
3	Vitamin D (µg)	0.1
4	Magnesium (mg)	37
5	Vitamin A (RE)	185
6	B_{12} (µg)	0.12
7	Zinc (mg)	0.6
8	Thiamin (mg)	0.16
9	Riboflavin (mg)	0.1
10	Niacin (NE)	2.78

TIP: To increase the protein content, bring along some hard-boiled eggs in the cooler and add to the salad just before serving.

Kitchen Sink Salad

TIP: You could also make this salad using apples and kiwis.

Yogurt is a great way to increase your calcium intake, and yogurt-based dressings have considerably fewer calories. To steal a phrase, that's a good thing.

Serves 6

1	romaine lettuce, rinsed, patted dry and torn in pieces	1
12	orange segments, cut in half	12
1	banana, peeled and sliced	1
1/2	red onion, sliced	1
12	cooked large shrimp, shelled and cut lengthwise	12
1/3 cup	blanched pistachios	75 mL

Yogurt and Curry Dressing

2/3 cup	plain yogurt	150 mL
3 tbsp	mayonnaise	45 mL
2 tbsp	lime juice	30 mL
2 tsp	curry powder	10 mL
	Pepper	

1. *Prepare Yogurt and Curry Dressing:* In a small bowl combine all dressing ingredients and season to taste with pepper.

2. In a large salad bowl, combine lettuce, oranges, banana and onion. Toss with Yogurt and Curry Dressing.

3. Serve salad in 4 to 6 salad bowls and top with shrimp and pistachios.

Vegetables and Sides

Cheesy Mashed Potatoes

Garlicky Beans with Toasted Almonds

Honeyed Peas and Carrots

Ratatouille with Havarti

Vegetable and Cheddar Frittata

Rice Primavera

Spinach Rice with Feta

Cauliflower Bake

Cheesy Mashed Potatoes

PER SERVING	
Calories	320
Protein (g)	9.2
Carbohydrates (g)	33
Fat (g)	17.3
Sat	10.8
Mono	4.9
Poly	0.6

TOP 10		
1	Calcium (mg)	208
2	Potassium (mg)	580
3	Vitamin D (µg)	0.5
4	Magnesium (mg)	41
5	Vitamin A (RE)	160
6	B$_{12}$ (µg)	0.23
7	Zinc (mg)	1.2
8	Thiamin (mg)	0.17
9	Riboflavin (mg)	0.16
10	Niacin (NE)	4.24

TIP: You could use almost any cheese here...the possibilities are endless.

Just a cheesy way of getting more calcium into the family's diet—and remember, every family member needs it.

Serves 5

6	all-purpose potatoes, peeled and quartered	6
1/2 cup	warm milk	125 mL
1/4 cup	butter, softened	50 mL
1 cup	shredded cheddar cheese	250 mL
	Salt and pepper	

1. In a large saucepan, cook potatoes in boiling salted water for 20 minutes, or until tender; drain.

2. Mash potatoes; add milk and butter.

3. Stir in cheddar cheese. Season with salt and pepper to taste and serve immediately.

Garlicky Beans with Toasted Almonds

The garlic and tomatoes in this recipe give it a Mediterranean twist. Green and wax beans are low in calories, but still nutritious.

Serves 8

Preheat broiler

1/2 cup	sliced almonds	125 mL
3 tbsp	butter	45 mL
3	garlic cloves, crushed	3
2	tomatoes, trimmed and diced	2
1 lb	green and wax beans	500 g
1 tbsp	liquid honey	15 mL
	Juice of 1/2 lime	
	Salt and pepper	

1. Toast almonds under broiler for at least 1 minute until golden.

2. In a saucepan of boiling water, cook beans for a few minutes until tender-crisp. Drain and set aside.

3. In a large saucepan, sauté garlic and tomatoes in butter for 2 minutes. Stir in beans, honey and lime juice. Season to taste with salt and pepper. Turn heat off, cover and let stand for 4 minutes.

4. Serve immediately, topped with toasted almonds.

PER SERVING	
Calories	112
Protein (g)	2.9
Carbohydrates (g)	9.8
Fat (g)	7.9
Sat	3
Mono	3.4
Poly	1.1

TOP 10		
1	Calcium (mg)	46
2	Potassium (mg)	285
3	Vitamin D (μg)	0.1
4	Magnesium (mg)	36
5	Vitamin A (RE)	110
6	B_{12} (μg)	0.01
7	Zinc (mg)	0.5
8	Thiamin (mg)	0.07
9	Riboflavin (mg)	0.11
10	Niacin (NE)	1.22

TIP: For a change of pace, use toasted sesame seeds or even pecans.

Honeyed Peas and Carrots

PER SERVING	
Calories	219
Protein (g)	4.9
Carbohydrates (g)	34.4
Fat (g)	8.1
Sat	4.9
Mono	2.2
Poly	0.5

TOP 10		
1	Calcium (mg)	58
2	Potassium (mg)	411
3	Vitamin D (µg)	0.1
4	Magnesium (mg)	36
5	Vitamin A (RE)	3189
6	B_{12} (µg)	0.01
7	Zinc (mg)	1
8	Thiamin (mg)	0.23
9	Riboflavin (mg)	0.15
10	Niacin (NE)	2.32

There's something terribly old-fashioned about peas and carrots, but add a little honey and basil, and presto—gourmet!

Serves 6

2 lbs	carrots, cut into sticks	1 kg
1 lb	fresh or frozen green peas, thawed	500 g
4 tbsp	honey	60 mL
4 tbsp	butter	60 mL
2 tbsp	lemon juice	30 mL
	Dried basil	
	Salt and pepper	

1. Peel carrots and cook in boiling water in a large saucepot until tender-crisp. Drain and stir in green peas, honey, butter and lemon juice. Heat over low heat for 5 minutes, stirring constantly.

2. Season to taste with basil, salt and pepper, and serve immediately.

TIP: Raw carrots are great, but you actually get a bit more beta carotene from the cooked carrot, as cooking ruptures the cells and makes the nutrient more available for absorption. Who'da thunk it?

Ratatouille with Havarti

You probably know how to pronounce this, but just in case, the "touille" part rhymes with phooey: rata-tooey. However you say it, you get a boatload of nutrients with this dish. The cheese adds calcium and other nutrients, plus protein and some fat to help you absorb the fat-soluble vitamins.

Serves 4

Preheat oven to 425°F (220°C)
2 ovenproof dishes and a baking sheet

1	eggplant, sliced into rounds	1
2	zucchini, sliced into rounds	2
2	bell peppers (red and/or yellow), seeded and quartered	2
1	large onion, sliced into thick rounds	1
2	large carrots, sliced into sticks	2
4	tomatoes, halved	4
1/4 cup	virgin olive oil	60 mL
	Salt and pepper	
3 tbsp	pine nuts	45 mL
3 tbsp	chopped fresh parsley	45 mL
5 oz	Havarti cheese, in thin slices	150 g

1. Place eggplant slices in a colander and sprinkle with a little salt. Let stand for about 20 minutes to extract moisture. Rinse thoroughly, drain and dry with paper towels.

2. Brush all vegetables with a little olive oil and place in ovenproof dishes. Roast in preheated oven for about 20 minutes, or until lightly browned and bell pepper skin starts to blister. Reduce oven temperature to 350°F (180°C).

3. Transfer vegetables to a large dish (peel skin off peppers if desired). Moisten with cooking juices, season with salt and pepper. Let cool.

4. Scatter pine nuts on baking sheet and roast for 7 to 8 minutes.

5. When vegetables have cooled to room temperature, mix in parsley and roasted pine nuts. Distribute Havarti slices over ratatouille.

PER SERVING	
Calories	408
Protein (g)	14.9
Carbohydrates (g)	29.5
Fat (g)	28
Sat	8.9
Mono	14.3
Poly	3.3

TOP 10		
1	Calcium (mg)	311
2	Potassium (mg)	1076
3	Vitamin D (μg)	–
4	Magnesium (mg)	90
5	Vitamin A (RE)	1585
6	B_{12} (μg)	0.55
7	Zinc (mg)	2.5
8	Thiamin (mg)	0.32
9	Riboflavin (mg)	0.3
10	Niacin (NE)	5.77

TIP: Serve as an appetizer with crusty bread or as an accompaniment to grilled meat.

Vegetable and Cheddar Frittata

TIP: Frozen vegetables are as nutritious as their fresh counterparts—and are sometimes more so. The fresh ones sometimes have a long trip to your grocery store (even as much as a couple of weeks!) and then hang around there, losing nutrients. The frozen ones, on the other hand, are frozen at their peak of ripeness, when nutrient content is at its highest.

Another great way to slip some veggies to those who are low in this food group; also a way to use up those frozen packages hiding out in the back or bottom of the freezer.

Serves 4

4 cups	frozen mixed vegetables	1 L
6	eggs	6
1/2 tsp	salt	2 mL
1/2 tsp	dried basil	2 mL
	Pepper	
2 tbsp	vegetable oil	30 mL
2	cloves garlic, minced	2
1	medium onion, sliced	1
1 cup	cheddar or Swiss cheese	250 mL

1. In a medium saucepan, bring 2 cups (500 mL) salted water to boil. Add frozen vegetables and cover. When water returns to a boil, drain vegetables in a colander. Cut larger pieces of vegetable.

2. Beat together eggs, salt, basil and pepper until just blended.

3. Heat oil in 10-inch (25 cm) nonstick skillet over medium heat. Add garlic and onion. Sauté until onion is tender, about 3 minutes. Add vegetables. Sauté until vegetables are hot.

4. Pour eggs over vegetables in skillet. Reduce heat to medium-low. Cover and cook until eggs are almost set. Sprinkle with cheese. Leave on the burner until cheese melts, about 1 minute.

The Everyday Calcium Cookbook

Rice Primavera

Most people have heard of, or tried, pasta primavera, which is basically pasta with a tomato-based vegetable sauce. No reason in the world not to have this sauce on rice—and it's delicious.

Serves 8

¼ cup	butter	50 mL
¼ tsp	dried oregano leaves, crushed	1 mL
¼ tsp	dried basil leaves, crushed	1 mL
¼ tsp	garlic powder	1 mL
¼ cup	chopped onion	50 mL
1½ cups	sliced zucchini (about 1 medium)	375 mL
1 cup	sliced mushrooms	250 mL
1 cup	whole kernel corn	250 mL
2 cups	cooked rice	500 mL
1 cup	dried seeded tomatoes	250 mL
	Salt and pepper	

1. Melt butter in a large nonstick skillet. Stir in oregano, basil and garlic powder. Add onion; sauté for 2 to 3 minutes.

2. Add zucchini, mushrooms and corn. Cook and stir, uncovered, over medium heat until vegetables are tender and any liquid has evaporated.

3. Add rice and tomatoes. Cook and stir until heated through. Add salt and pepper to taste.

PER SERVING	
Calories	161
Protein (g)	3.5
Carbohydrates (g)	24.5
Fat (g)	6.3
Sat	3.7
Mono	1.8
Poly	0.4

TOP 10		
1	Calcium (mg)	21
2	Potassium (mg)	406
3	Vitamin D (µg)	0.1
4	Magnesium (mg)	32
5	Vitamin A (RE)	70
6	B_{12} (µg)	0.01
7	Zinc (mg)	0.6
8	Thiamin (mg)	0.08
9	Riboflavin (mg)	0.09
10	Niacin (NE)	2.17

TIP: If you're concerned about your fiber intake (and you should be), then use brown rice instead of white. It has the same nutty flavor as whole-grain pasta.

Spinach Rice with Feta

This flexible dish also tastes delicious cold!

Serves 6

1 tbsp	butter	15 mL
2	garlic cloves, chopped	2
2	celery stalks, sliced	2
1	red onion, chopped	1
1 cup	sliced mushrooms	250 mL
	Juice of ½ lemon	
2 cups	water	500 mL
1 cup	white rice	250 mL
3 cups	chopped spinach	750 mL
4 oz	feta cheese, diced	120 g
	Salt and pepper	
	Cumin	
	Dried oregano	

1. Melt butter in a large saucepan; sauté garlic, celery, onion and mushrooms. Sprinkle with lemon juice and cook for 2 minutes.

2. Add water and rice; bring to boil. Cover and cook over low heat until rice is done. Remove from heat.

3. Stir in spinach. Cover and let rest for 10 minutes.

4. Add feta cheese and season to taste with salt, pepper, cumin and oregano. Toss and serve immediately.

Cauliflower Bake

You can choose to make this with broccoli, and it will be more colorful, but the taste with the cauliflower is exceptional. And it's a good way to increase both calcium and veggie intake.

Serves 6

Preheat oven to 350°F (180°C)
8-cup (2 L) casserole dish

1	large head cauliflower and/or broccoli, cut into florets	1
¼ cup	butter	50 mL
2 cups	sliced fresh mushrooms	500 mL
⅓ cup	finely chopped celery (about 1 medium rib)	75 mL
2 tbsp	flour	30 mL
¼ tsp	dry mustard	1 mL
1¼ cups	milk	300 mL
1 cup	shredded Swiss cheese	250 mL
	Salt and pepper	
½ cup	cornflake crumbs	125 mL
2 tbsp	melted butter	30 mL

PER SERVING	
Calories	276
Protein (g)	10.6
Carbohydrates (g)	18.9
Fat (g)	18.4
Sat	11.2
Mono	5
Poly	0.9

TOP 10		
1	Calcium (mg)	269
2	Potassium (mg)	350
3	Vitamin D (µg)	0.9
4	Magnesium (mg)	28
5	Vitamin A (RE)	182
6	B_{12} (µg)	0.39
7	Zinc (mg)	1.3
8	Thiamin (mg)	0.29
9	Riboflavin (mg)	0.54
10	Niacin (NE)	4.32

1. In a large saucepan, cook cauliflower in boiling salted water until tender-crisp; drain.

2. In a medium saucepan, melt the ¼ cup (50 mL) butter. Sauté mushrooms and celery until tender and liquid has evaporated. Blend in flour and dry mustard. Gradually stir in milk. Cook and stir over medium heat until mixture boils and thickens. Remove from heat, add Swiss cheese and stir until cheese is melted. Season with salt and pepper to taste.

3. Place cauliflower in casserole dish and pour sauce over top. Combine cornflake crumbs and melted butter; sprinkle over casserole. Bake in preheated oven for 20 minutes, or until heated through.

TIP: Toasted nuts (almonds or walnuts) add another dimension to this dish, as well as extra nutrients.

Casseroles

Fish au Gratin

Chicken Casserole au Gratin

Noodle Casserole

Linguini Pomodoro with Crisp Bacon

Pasta Italiano

Turkey and Potato Casserole

Country Strata au Gratin

Mixed Seafood Casserole

Fettuccini and Cheese with Sun-Dried Tomatoes

Turkey Quiche

Bean and Sausage Cassoulet

Fish au Gratin

This is a fish dish for people who think they hate fish. It's bound to make a believer out of them. The beauty of cheese on a dish is not just that it increases the nutrient quotient, but it also encourages people to eat something they otherwise might avoid—like fish or broccoli! An excellent source of calcium.

PER SERVING	
Calories	490
Protein (g)	34.2
Carbohydrates (g)	44
Fat (g)	19.1
Sat	10.7
Mono	5.3
Poly	1.4

TOP 10		
1	Calcium (mg)	298
2	Potassium (mg)	565
3	Vitamin D (µg)	1.7
4	Magnesium (mg)	77
5	Vitamin A (RE)	180
6	B_{12} (µg)	1.25
7	Zinc (mg)	2.5
8	Thiamin (mg)	0.15
9	Riboflavin (mg)	0.29
10	Niacin (NE)	9.69

Tip: Try lime juice instead of lemon, and serve with lime wedges.

Serves 4

Preheat oven to 450°F (220°C)
Baking sheet

1	package (14 oz/400 g) frozen cod, haddock or sole fillets	1
2 tbsp	butter, divided	30 mL
2 tsp	lemon juice	10 mL
	Salt	
	Paprika	
	Hot cooked noodles or rice	
1 tbsp	flour	15 mL
1/4 tsp	dry mustard	1 mL
3/4 cup	milk	175 mL
1 cup	shredded cheddar cheese	250 mL
1 tbsp	chopped fresh parsley	15 mL
	Salt and pepper	

1. Cut frozen fish crosswise into 4 pieces. Place fillets on large piece of foil, shiny side up. Dot fish with 1 tbsp (15 mL) of butter. Sprinkle with lemon juice, salt and paprika. Bring edges of foil together; fold to seal. Place on baking sheet.

2. Bake in preheated oven for 30 minutes, or until fish flakes with fork. Drain fish, reserving 1/3 cup (75 mL) liquid in foil. Arrange cooked fish on noodles; keep warm.

3. In a medium saucepan, melt remaining 1 tbsp (15 mL) butter. Blend in flour and mustard. Gradually stir in milk and reserved fish liquid. Cook and stir over medium heat until mixture boils and thickens. Remove from heat.

4. Add cheddar cheese and stir until cheese is melted. Add parsley and salt and pepper to taste. To serve, pour sauce over fish and noodles.

Chicken Casserole au Gratin

The great thing about casseroles is that you get all the food groups in one dish. I'd still serve a salad along with this, since we all struggle to get enough fruits and veggies in our diets.

Serves 4

Preheat oven to 350°F (180°C)
Large casserole dish

2 tbsp	softened butter, divided	30 mL
1½ lb	boneless chicken breasts	750 g
⅓ cup	dry white wine	75 mL
1½ cup	chicken broth	375 mL
1 tsp	dried tarragon	5 mL
2	whole cloves (optional)	2
1	onion, chopped	1
1	garlic clove, minced	1
	Salt and pepper	
4 cups	tortiglioni (or any other short pasta)	1 L
2 cups	broccoli florets	500 mL
2 tbsp	all-purpose flour	30 mL
½ lb	Havarti cheese, shredded	250 g
¾ cup	breadcrumbs	200 mL

1. Melt half the butter in a large saucepan over medium heat, add chicken and brown on both sides. Pour in wine and chicken broth, add tarragon, cloves, (if using), onion, garlic and salt and pepper to taste. Bring to a boil over high heat. Cover and let simmer over low heat for about 20 to 25 minutes, until chicken is tender.

2. Meanwhile, cook the tortiglioni according to instructions on package, adding broccoli florets to the cooking water with pasta. Drain and set aside.

3. Remove the chicken from the pan and dice. Keep warm.

4. Mix together the remaining butter and the flour. Stir mixture into remaining juices in saucepan. Bring to a boil over medium heat, stirring constantly.

PER SERVING	
Calories	886
Protein (g)	69.4
Carbohydrates (g)	85
Fat (g)	27.6
Sat	15.1
Mono	7.7
Poly	2.2

TOP 10		
1	Calcium (mg)	500
2	Potassium (mg)	884
3	Vitamin D (µg)	0.1
4	Magnesium (mg)	126
5	Vitamin A (RE)	195
6	B_{12} (µg)	1.41
7	Zinc (mg)	5.3
8	Thiamin (mg)	0.65
9	Riboflavin (mg)	0.57
10	Niacin (NE)	32.66

TIP: If you don't want to put wine in this casserole, or you just don't want to open a bottle for a third of a cup, then use apple juice; it works just as well.

5.   Remove from heat and gently stir in tortiglioni, broccoli and chicken. Pour into casserole dish and top with shredded Havarti cheese and breadcrumbs.

6.   Bake in preheated oven for 8 to 10 minutes, until golden brown. Serve hot.

Noodle Casserole

This dish does away with the problem of fiddling with lasagna noodles—this recipe is a breeze to make!

Serves 6

Preheat oven to 350°F (180°C)
8-inch (2 L) square baking dish

3 cups	medium-sized noodles	750 mL
1 lb	lean ground beef	500 g
1/2 cup	chopped green peppers (about 1/2 medium)	125 mL
1	can (14 oz/398 mL) tomato sauce	1
1/2 tsp	dried oregano	2 mL
1 cup	cottage cheese	250 mL
1 cup	shredded cheddar cheese, divided	250 mL
1/4 cup	sour cream	50 mL
2 tbsp	finely chopped green onions (about 1 medium)	30 mL
1/2 tsp	salt	2 mL

1. In a large saucepan, cook noodles according to package directions; drain.

2. In a large nonstick skillet, sauté beef and green pepper until meat is browned and green pepper is tender; drain.

3. Stir in tomato sauce and oregano. Over medium heat, bring mixture to a boil, stirring constantly. Remove from heat and set aside.

4. In a small bowl, combine cottage cheese, half of the cheddar cheese, sour cream, green onions and salt.

5. Layer half of the noodles in baking dish. Cover with cheese mixture. Layer remaining noodles and top with meat sauce. Sprinkle remaining 1/2 cup (125 mL) of cheddar cheese over meat sauce. Bake in preheated oven, uncovered, for 30 minutes or until heated through. Let stand 5 minutes before serving.

PER SERVING	
Calories	378
Protein (g)	28.6
Carbohydrates (g)	21.4
Fat (g)	19.6
Sat	9.6
Mono	7.2
Poly	0.8

TOP 10		
1	Calcium (mg)	199
2	Potassium (mg)	567
3	Vitamin D (µg)	0.1
4	Magnesium (mg)	48
5	Vitamin A (RE)	144
6	B₁₂ (µg)	1.62
7	Zinc (mg)	4.8
8	Thiamin (mg)	0.13
9	Riboflavin (mg)	0.38
10	Niacin (NE)	10.57

TIP: Use whole-grain noodles when making this dish—it's a painless way to increase fiber intake.

Linguini Pomodoro with Crisp Bacon

TIP: If you really want to make this fancy, use pancetta (Italian bacon) in place of the regular bacon.

Pomodoro is Italian for tomato, but the Italian word makes it sound classier than "linguini with tomatoes." You can give it a Gaelic name if you like; it will still be a great addition to your recipe repertoire.

Serves 6

¼ lb	side bacon	125 g
3	cloves garlic, minced	3
1	large onion, chopped	1
1	can (28 oz/796 mL) plum tomatoes, with juice	1
1 to 2 tbsp	soy sauce	15 to 30 mL
1 tsp	dried basil leaves	5 mL
1	package (15 oz/450 g) linguini	1
½ cup	chopped fresh parsley	125 mL
1 cup	diced mozzarella	250 mL
⅓ cup	grated Parmesan	75 mL
	Hot chili pepper flakes	

1. Cook bacon in a large saucepan over medium-high heat until crisp. Drain, reserving 3 tbsp (45 mL) drippings; crumble bacon into small bits and set aside.

2. Return reserved drippings to pan. Add garlic and onion and sauté over medium-high heat until softened.

3. Add tomatoes with their juice, breaking tomatoes up with a fork. Add soy sauce and basil. Bring to a boil, reduce heat and simmer, uncovered, for 10 minutes.

4. Meanwhile, cook linguini according to package directions; drain and place in a large pasta bowl.

5. Stir parsley into sauce and pour over linguini; toss well to coat.

6. Divide pasta among individual serving bowls; sprinkle each with mozzarella, cooked bacon, Parmesan and hot pepper flakes to taste.

Easy Cheddar Biscuits (page 44)

Ham, Cheese and Asparagus Crêpes (page 36)

Overnight Cheddar Bagel Casserole (page 43)

Pesto Bruschetta on Focaccia (page 47); Garlic Crostini with Caramelized Onions (pages 48–49)

Creamy Herb Dip (page 55)

Creamy French Onion Soup (page 61)

Fabulous Feta Salad (page 69)

Garlicky Beans with Toasted Almonds (page 79)

Country Strata au Gratin (page 95)

Pasta Italiano (page 93)

Mixed Seafood Casserole (page 96)

Chocolate Banana Bread (page 109)

Honey Almond Cake (page 116)

Pasta Italiano

I suppose it's stating the obvious to describe pasta as Italian, but one of my Italian friends observed that this was a "true" Italian dish and should be described as such. I use fusilli when I make it. An excellent source of calcium.

Serves 6

Preheat oven to 350°F (180°C)
8-cup (2 L) shallow baking dish

4 cups	short pasta	375 mL
1 lb	lean ground beef	450 g
3/4 cup	chopped onion (about 1 medium)	175 mL
1/2 cup	chopped green pepper (about 1/2 medium)	125 mL
1/2 cup	tomato sauce	125 mL
1 tsp	dried basil leaves	5 mL
1 tsp	dried oregano leaves	5 mL
6 tbsp	butter, divided	90 mL
/4 cup	all-purpose flour	50 mL
1 tsp	dry mustard	5 mL
2 cups	milk	500 mL
3 cups	shredded cheddar, mozzarella or fontina cheese	750 mL
1 cup	fresh breadcrumbs	(250 mL)

PER SERVING	
Calories	788
Protein (g)	40.5
Carbohydrates (g)	57.4
Fat (g)	43.6
Sat	24.4
Mono	13.9
Poly	1.8

TOP 10		
1	Calcium (mg)	549
2	Potassium (mg)	579
3	Vitamin D (µg)	1.2
4	Magnesium (mg)	78
5	Vitamin A (RE)	331
6	B_{12} (µg)	1.91
7	Zinc (mg)	6.5
8	Thiamin (mg)	0.4
9	Riboflavin (mg)	0.63
10	Niacin (NE)	13.88

1. Cook pasta according to package directions. Drain and set aside.

2. Meanwhile, cook beef, onion and green pepper in a large nonstick skillet over medium-high heat until meat is browned; drain off fat.

3. Stir in tomato sauce, basil and oregano. Simmer for 3 minutes. Spoon into baking dish; set aside.

4. Melt 4 tbsp (60 mL) of the butter in a medium saucepan. Blend in flour and mustard. Gradually stir in milk. Cook over medium heat, stirring constantly, until mixture boils and thickens. Remove from heat.

5. Add cheese and stir until melted. Stir in cooked pasta. Spoon pasta and cheese over meat layer in baking dish.

6. Melt remaining 2 tbsp (30 mL) butter; combine with breadcrumbs. Sprinkle over pasta and cheese layer. Bake in preheated oven for 15 to 20 minutes or until hot and bubbly.

TIP: There's a lot of scientific evidence that a substance called lycopene (abundant in processed tomatoes and tomato sauce) reduces the risk of prostate cancer. That, plus the protection from conjugated linoleic acid (CLA) found in dairy fat, makes this a very healthful dish!

Turkey and Potato Casserole

TIP: Serve with creamy coleslaw.

Turkey shouldn't be just for Christmas and Thanksgiving. . . . It's great all year round. This recipe is terrific for the inevitable leftovers. An excellent source of calcium.

Serves 6

Preheat oven to 375°F (190°C)
Large casserole dish

4	large potatoes, peeled and sliced	4
2	white onions, sliced	2
2	garlic cloves, finely chopped	2
3 to 4 cups	cooked turkey chunks	750 mL to 1 L
6 tbsp	butter	90 mL
	Salt and pepper	
Pinch	grated nutmeg	Pinch
	All-purpose flour	
1 cup	table (15% or 18%) cream	250 mL
2 cups	grated Emmenthal cheese	500 mL

1. In a large ovenproof dish, layer alternately half the potato, half the onions and half the garlic.

2. Top with half the turkey and brush with 3 tbsp (45 mL) butter. Season to taste with salt and pepper. Sprinkle with nutmeg, flour and half the cream.

3. Repeat process with the other half of the ingredients, layering potato, onions, garlic and turkey, brushing with butter, seasoning with salt and pepper and sprinkling with nutmeg, flour and the remaining cream. Top with cheese.

4. Cover and bake in preheated oven for 45 minutes, or until potatoes are tender. Remove from oven and cool for 10 minutes before serving.

Country Strata au Gratin

Dinner doesn't get any more wholesome than this. An excellent source of calcium.

Serves 6

Preheat oven to 375°F (190°C)
8-cup (2 L) baking dish

4¹/₂ cups	potatoes, thinly sliced (about 1.25 lb)	1.125 L
2¹/₂ cups	grated Swiss cheese, divided	625 mL
1¹/₂ cups	onion, finely chopped (about 2 medium)	375 mL
2 tbsp	all-purpose flour	30 mL
¹/₂ tsp	salt	2 mL
¹/₂ tsp	pepper	2 mL
6 oz	thinly sliced ham	170 g
3 cups	broccoli, chopped	750 mL
1¹/₄ cups	milk	300 mL

1. In a baking dish, layer, in order:
   - Half the potatoes, with ²/₃ cup (160 mL) cheese mixed in
   - Half the onion
   - Half the flour, salt and pepper
   - All the ham
   - All the broccoli
   - Remaining potato, with ²/₃ cup (160 mL) cheese mixed in
   - Remaining onion, flour and seasonings

2. Pour milk over top. Cover with remaining cheese.

3. Bake in preheated oven, uncovered, until potatoes are fork-tender, about 60 to 90 minutes.

PER SERVING	
Calories	338
Protein (g)	24.2
Carbohydrates (g)	26.1
Fat (g)	15.6
Sat	9.5
Mono	4.4
Poly	0.8

TOP 10		
1	Calcium (mg)	551
2	Potassium (mg)	842
3	Vitamin D (µg)	1
4	Magnesium (mg)	60
5	Vitamin A (RE)	205
6	B₁₂ (µg)	1.06
7	Zinc (mg)	3.1
8	Thiamin (mg)	0.4
9	Riboflavin (mg)	0.41
10	Niacin (NE)	8.46

Mixed Seafood Casserole

TIP: While it's true that shrimp contain a lot of cholesterol, it's now known that the cholesterol in your food (dietary cholesterol) has relatively little impact on the level of cholesterol in your blood.

I've used shrimp and scallops here, but you can use any shellfish you like—even lobster if you're feeling flush! An excellent source of calcium.

Serves 6

Preheat broiler
6 individual baking dishes

4 tbsp	butter, divided	60 mL
2 cups	sliced mushrooms	500 mL
1/2	medium onion, finely chopped	1/2
1¼ lbs	fresh or frozen large shrimp, peeled and deveined	550 g
1¼ lbs	fresh or frozen small scallops	550 g
1 cup	dry white wine	250 mL
1/4 tsp	dried thyme leaves, crushed	1 mL
3 tbsp	all-purpose flour	45 mL
1 cup	milk	250 mL
1½ cups	shredded sharp cheddar, divided	375 mL
	Salt and pepper	
2 cups	coarsely torn sourdough or baguette bread	500 mL

1. Melt 1 tbsp (15 mL) butter in a large nonstick saucepan over medium-high heat. Add mushrooms and onion; cook and stir until tender.

2. Add shrimp, scallops, wine and thyme to the pan. Bring to boil, reduce heat and simmer 2 minutes, or until seafood is cooked. Drain, reserving 1 cup (250 mL) broth. Set seafood mixture aside.

3. Melt 2 tbsp (30 mL) more butter in the same pan. Remove from heat and blend in flour; gradually stir in reserved broth and milk. Cook and stir over medium-high heat until mixture boils and thickens.

4. Remove from heat, add 1 cup (250 mL) of sharp cheddar and stir until melted. Fold in cooked seafood mixture. Add salt and pepper to taste.

5. Melt remaining 1 tbsp (15 mL) butter and toss with torn bread and remaining ½ cup (125 mL) sharp cheddar.

6. Spoon seafood mixture into 6 individual baking dishes, sprinkle with cheese and bread mixture and broil until topping is toasted.

Variation

Reduce seafood to 1 lb (450 g) each of shrimp and scallops. Cook and stir ½ cup (125 mL) each chopped green pepper and celery in a little butter. Add ¾ cup (175 mL) diced seeded tomato and cook until heated through. Fold into cheese sauce along with seafood mixture. Season to taste with hot pepper sauce or cayenne pepper. Serve over hot cooked rice or pasta.

Fettuccini and Cheese with Sun-Dried Tomatoes

TIP: Serve this with roasted vegetables cooked at the same time as the casserole.

For me, sun-dried tomatoes were an acquired taste; now I can't get enough of them. It's interesting that so many Mediterranean-type recipes use some combination of cheese and tomatoes. That probably helps explain the good health of the people who live on the Mediterranean. An excellent source of calcium.

Serves 10

Heat oven to 325°F (180°C)
8-inch (2 L) square baking dish, buttered, and large baking pan

1 cup	sun-dried tomatoes	250 mL
3 cups	whipping (35%) cream	750 mL
1 lb	fettuccini	450 g
2 tbsp	butter	30 mL
8	eggs	8
	Salt and pepper	
¹/₂ lb	mozzarella cheese, cubed	250 g
¹/₂ lb	brick cheese, grated	250 g

1. If using oil-packed sun-dried tomatoes, drain and pat dry. If using dry ones, put them in 1 cup (250 mL) of the cream to soften for 20 minutes. Reserving cream, drain tomatoes, chop coarsely and put into a mixing bowl.

2. Cook pasta al dente. Drain. Put pasta in a bowl and toss with butter and sun-dried tomatoes.

3. Combine cream, eggs, salt and pepper in another bowl. If more liquid is needed, use up to 1 cup (250 mL) more of half-and-half (10%) cream or milk. Beat well.

4. Add mozzarella and brick cheese to noodles. Mix well. Add cream mixture and pour into baking dish.

5. Cover dish with foil. Put into a large pan filled with boiling water (a *bain-marie*) and cook in oven until set, 30 to 40 minutes. Take the dish out of the *bain-marie* and let stand 5 to 10 minutes before serving.

Turkey Quiche

No "real men" jokes here except to point out that real men eat anything they want ... especially a quiche as good as this one. An excellent source of calcium.

Serves 6

Preheat oven to 375°F (190°C)
Baking sheet

2 cups	shredded Swiss cheese	500 mL
1 cup	chopped, cooked turkey	250 mL
1 tbsp	finely chopped green onion	15 mL
1 tbsp	finely chopped celery	15 mL
1 tbsp	finely chopped parsley	15 mL
1 tbsp	all-purpose flour	15 mL
1/2 tsp	salt	2 mL
3	eggs	3
1 cup	half-and-half (10%) cream	250 mL
1	unbaked pie shell (9-inch/23 cm)	1
1 tbsp	grated Canadian Parmesan cheese	15 mL

1. In a medium bowl, toss together Swiss cheese, turkey, onion, celery, parsley, flour and salt.

2. In a large bowl, beat eggs lightly; gradually stir in cream. Add cheese and turkey mixture; stir to combine. Pour into pie shell and place shell on baking sheet. Sprinkle with Canadian Parmesan cheese.

3. Bake in preheated oven for 30 to 35 minutes, or until knife or toothpick inserted in center comes out clean.

PER SERVING	
Calories	383
Protein (g)	23.4
Carbohydrates (g)	14.8
Fat (g)	25.2
Sat	12.8
Mono	8.5
Poly	2.1

TOP 10		
1	Calcium (mg)	445
2	Potassium (mg)	233
3	Vitamin D (µg)	0.6
4	Magnesium (mg)	31
5	Vitamin A (RE)	173
6	B_{12} (µg)	1.03
7	Zinc (mg)	2.8
8	Thiamin (mg)	0.12
9	Riboflavin (mg)	0.42
10	Niacin (NE)	7.18

TIP: This dish also tastes great made with chicken.

Bean and Sausage Cassoulet

TIP: If you anticipate a family revolt against the use of lima beans, use pinto beans or chickpeas.

TIP: You can vary this recipe by using Italian sausage—mild or spicy.

Traditionally, cassoulet is made with white beans and some form of pork and sausage. The term "cassoulet" comes from the glazed, earthenware container in which the dish was originally cooked.

Serves 12

Preheat oven to 350°F (180°C)
16-cup (4 L) baking dish

1½ lbs	Polish sausage	750 g
2	cans (each 14 oz/398 mL) baked beans	2
2	cans (each 14 oz/398 mL) red kidney beans, drained	2
1	can (14 oz/398 mL) lima beans, drained	1
3 cups	shredded cheddar cheese	750 mL
1	can (7.5 oz/213 mL) tomato sauce	1
⅓ cup	molasses	75 mL
2 tsp	onion salt	10 mL
½ tsp	ground black pepper	2 mL
¼ tsp	dry mustard	1 mL

1. Remove casing from sausage and cut into ½-inch (1 cm) thick slices.

2. In baking dish, combine baked beans, kidney beans, lima beans, sausage and cheddar cheese.

3. In a small bowl, combine tomato sauce, molasses, onion salt, pepper and dry mustard; pour over beans and stir to combine.

4. Bake in preheated oven, uncovered, for 1 hour. Stir and bake for 15 minutes longer.

Desserts

Raspberry Coulis Cheesecake

Grilled Fruit Kabobs with Tangy Lemon Yogurt Sauce

Fruity Dessert Crunch

Fruit Quesadillas

Chocolate Banana Bread

Summery Strawberry Rhubarb Cake

Almond Butterscotch Bars

Strawberry Trifle

Fresh Fruit Pizza

Fabulous Rice Pudding

Honey Almond Cake

Amazing Berries 'n' Cream Mille Feuille

Raspberry Coulis Cheesecake

TIP: You could also make a strawberry or blueberry coulis.

You might well wonder how a nutritionist has the gall to include a recipe for cheesecake. It's because this nutritionist believes in the pleasure principle and portion control. Have the pleasure . . . just control yourself!

Serves 8

Preheat oven to 325°F (160°C)
9-inch (23 cm) springform pan, buttered

1 cup	finely crushed butter cookies (about 22 cookies)	250 mL
½ cup	butter, melted	125 g
1 lb	cream cheese	500 g
⅔ cup	plain yogurt	150 mL
4 tbsp	liquid honey	60 mL
½ cup	granulated sugar	125 mL
4	eggs	4
1 tsp	vanilla	5 mL

Raspberry Coulis

1 tbsp	cornstarch	15 mL
¼ cup	water	50 mL
2 tbsp	granulated sugar	30 mL
1 cup	fresh raspberries	250 mL

1. In a medium bowl, combine crushed cookies and butter. Press into the bottom of the prepared pan.

2. In a large bowl, beat cream cheese with yogurt, honey, sugar, eggs and vanilla until smooth. Pour mixture over crust and bake in preheated oven for 75 minutes. Turn oven off and let cake stand for 15 minutes in oven. Remove from oven and let stand in pan for 30 minutes.

3. *Prepare Raspberry Coulis:* In a small bowl, blend 1 tbsp (15 mL) cornstarch with ¼ cup water (50 mL); set aside. In a saucepan, combine water, sugar and raspberries and bring to a boil. Stirring constantly, allow mixture to boil for 5 minutes. Stir in diluted cornstarch and boil for 2 minutes more, stirring

The Everyday Calcium Cookbook

constantly. Remove from heat and let cool for 30 to 60 minutes. Purée in blender until smooth. Strain (optional).

4. When cheesecake is cool, garnish with whole fresh raspberries and serve with Raspberry Coulis drizzled over the top.

Grilled Fruit Kabobs with Tangy Lemon Yogurt Sauce

TIP: If you are using wooden skewers, soak them in cold water for 30 minutes first.

This is one of the most nutritious desserts imaginable. Naturally, you can vary the fruits, but the ones below make an enticing combo.

Serves 6

Preheat barbecue or indoor grill

12	chunks peeled papaya	12
12	chunks banana	12
12	chunks mango	12
12	chunks pineapple	12
12	chunks kiwi	12
12	strawberries	12
¼ cup	butter, melted	50 mL
¼ cup	honey	50 mL
	Tangy Lemon Yogurt Sauce (see recipe)	

1. Thread fruit chunks and strawberries onto 12 skewers.

2. Combine butter and honey. Brush honey butter over kabobs.

3. Grill for 3 to 4 minutes per side, or until hot and glazed, brushing occasionally with honey butter.

4. Serve immediately with Tangy Lemon Yogurt Sauce.

Tangy Lemon Yogurt Sauce

Makes 2-½ cups (625 mL)

1	container (500 g) vanilla yogurt	1
⅓ cup	honey	75 mL
1½ tsp	grated lemon rind	7 mL
2 tbsp	lemon juice	30 mL

TIP: This sauce is excellent poured over any fresh fruit—well, maybe not lemons. Great on berries and with strawberry shortcake and angel food cake.

1. Combine yogurt, honey, lemon rind and lemon juice. Chill for 1 hour to blend flavors.

Fruity Dessert Crunch

PER SERVING	
Calories	321
Protein (g)	9.3
Carbohydrates (g)	51.7
Fat (g)	10.6
Sat	2
Mono	5.4
Poly	2.4

TOP 10

1	Calcium (mg)	177
2	Potassium (mg)	568
3	Vitamin D (µg)	0.3
4	Magnesium (mg)	89
5	Vitamin A (RE)	34
6	B$_{12}$ (µg)	0.28
7	Zinc (mg)	2.4
8	Thiamin (mg)	0.17
9	Riboflavin (mg)	0.34
10	Niacin (NE)	2.67

Ha! And you thought oatmeal was only for breakfast. This recipe's good for any meal, especially brunch.

Serves 4

2 oz	quick-cooking rolled oats	60 g
½ cup	milk, warmed	125 mL
6 oz	plain yogurt	175 g
4 tbsp	maple syrup	60 mL
1	red apple, washed, with peel	1
1	pear, washed, with peel	1
2½ cups	mixed berries	625 mL
2 oz	chopped almonds (or other nuts)	50 g
4	strawberries to garnish	4

1. Soak oats in warm milk for 15 minutes, then blend in yogurt and maple syrup.

2. Grate apple and pear and add to mixture.

3. Chop berries (if necessary) and add to mixture.

4. Add almonds or nuts.

5. Pour cream into glass serving dishes. Garnish with strawberries and mint leaves. Keeps 24 hours in refrigerator.

Fruit Quesadillas

This is an unusual recipe, which might explain why it's one of my favorites. Especially good for brunch or a light supper. An excellent source of calcium.

Serves 4

4	eggs	4
1/4 cup	milk	50 mL
1 tbsp	butter	15 mL
2	pears, rinsed, trimmed and cut in cubes	2
1 cup	strawberries, hulled and sliced	250 mL
1 tbsp	canola oil	15 mL
4	large (8-inch/20 cm) tortillas	4
1 cup	grated mild cheddar cheese	250 mL
	fresh mint leaves	
	red grapes	

Yogurt and Lemon Sweet Sauce

1 cup	plain yogurt	250 mL
1/2 tsp	almond extract	10 mL
1 tbsp	lemon juice	15 mL
3 tbsp	confectioner's (icing) sugar	45 mL

PER SERVING	
Calories	504
Protein (g)	20.8
Carbohydrates (g)	47.7
Fat (g)	26
Sat	11.6
Mono	9.6
Poly	2.8

TOP 10		
1	Calcium (mg)	375
2	Potassium (mg)	455
3	Vitamin D (µg)	0.7
4	Magnesium (mg)	44
5	Vitamin A (RE)	208
6	B_{12} (µg)	1.09
7	Zinc (mg)	2.3
8	Thiamin (mg)	0.32
9	Riboflavin (mg)	0.64
10	Niacin (NE)	6.06

1. *Prepare Yogurt and Lemon Sweet Sauce:* In a medium bowl, mix all ingredients until smooth. Set aside.

2. In a small bowl, whisk eggs with milk.

3. In a skillet, heat butter over medium heat and cook egg mixture for 3 minutes, stirring occasionally.

4. Pour into a large bowl and stir in pear and strawberries. Reserve few fruit pieces for garnish.

5. In large nonstick skillet, heat oil over medium heat. Place 1 tortilla in skillet and sprinkle with 1/4 cup (50 mL) cheddar cheese. Top with half the scrambled egg mixture and sprinkle again with 1/4 cup (50 mL) cheese. Top with other tortilla. Cook for 2 to 3 minutes, or until crisp. Gently turn over and cook for

TIP: If you haven't tried Asian or Nashi pears yet, this is a great way to use them. They're sort of a cross between an ordinary pear and an apple, but in my view, they're better than either.

another 2 minutes. Remove from skillet and keep warm. Repeat process with remaining tortillas, cheese and egg mixture.

6. Cut each quesadilla into 4 slices and serve 2 slices per person. Drizzle with Yogurt and Lemon Sweet Sauce. Garnish with fresh mint leaves and reserved fruit pieces. Serve with red grapes.

Chocolate Banana Bread

My daughter-in-law, Dianne, can whip up muffins or quick breads at the drop of a hat. This recipe has the best of all worlds: chocolate and banana. Have it with a glass of milk!

Serves 8

Preheat oven to 350°F (180°C)
9- × 5-inch (1.5 L) loaf pan, lightly buttered or sprayed

2¼ cups	all-purpose flour	550 mL
⅓ cup	sifted unsweetened cocoa powder	75 mL
1 tsp	baking powder	5 mL
1 tsp	baking soda	5 mL
¼ tsp	salt	1 mL
⅓ cup	butter, softened	75 mL
¾ cup	granulated sugar	175 mL
1 cup	mashed ripe banana (about 2 medium)	250 mL
2	eggs	2
2 tsp	vanilla	10 mL
1 cup	milk, soured, or buttermilk	250 mL
1 cup	walnut pieces	250 mL

1. In a medium bowl, combine flour, cocoa, baking powder, baking soda and salt.

2. In a separate large bowl, using electric mixer, beat butter and sugar until light and fluffy; beat in banana, eggs and vanilla.

3. Stir flour mixture into banana mixture alternately with milk, making 3 additions of flour and 2 of milk. Stir in walnuts. Spread into prepared pan.

4. Bake in preheated oven for 60 minutes, or until knife or toothpick inserted in center comes out clean. Let cool in pan on rack for 5 minutes. Turn out onto rack to cool completely.

PER SERVING	
Calories	438
Protein (g)	9.5
Carbohydrates (g)	58
Fat (g)	20.6
Sat	6.8
Mono	4.4
Poly	8

TOP 10		
1	Calcium (mg)	85
2	Potassium (mg)	372
3	Vitamin D (µg)	0.5
4	Magnesium (mg)	63
5	Vitamin A (RE)	108
6	B_{12} (µg)	0.17
7	Zinc (mg)	1.2
8	Thiamin (mg)	0.3
9	Riboflavin (mg)	0.32
10	Niacin (NE)	4.45

TIP: When bananas start to become over-ripe, put them in the freezer and use later in bread or muffin recipes.

Summery Strawberry Rhubarb Cake

Nothing says summer like strawberries and rhubard. A little decadent, but worth it.

Serves 8

Preheat oven to 350°F (180°C)
9-inch (23 cm) springform pan, buttered

¹/₂ cup	all-purpose flour	125 mL
1 tsp	baking powder	5 mL
Pinch	salt	Pinch
¹/₂ cup	granulated sugar	125 mL
2	egg yolks	2
¹/₄ cup	hot filtered coffee (liquid)	50 mL
¹/₂ tsp	vanilla	2 mL
2	egg whites	2

Strawberry Rhubarb Mousse

1 cup	sliced fresh rhubarb	250 mL
2 tbsp	granulated sugar	30 mL
1 cup	sliced fresh strawberries	250 mL
¹/₂ cup	sour cream	125 mL
¹/₄ lb	cream cheese	125 g
1	envelope unflavored gelatin	1
¹/₄ cup	pasteurized egg whites	50 mL
1 tbsp	confectioner's (icing) sugar	15 mL

Cream Cheese Icing

1	package (9 oz/250 g) cream cheese	1
4 tbsp	butter, softened	60 mL
6 tbsp	confectioner's (icing) sugar	90 mL
¹/₂ tsp	vanilla	2 mL

1. In a small bowl, combine flour, baking powder and salt; set aside.

2. In a medium bowl, beat sugar with egg yolks. Stir in coffee and vanilla.

3. Gradually beat flour mixture into egg yolk mixture with electric mixer, until smooth.

4. In a clean bowl, with clean beaters, beat egg whites until soft peaks form. Fold into egg-yolk mixture.

5. Pour mixture into prepared pan. Bake in preheated oven for 35 minutes, or until knife or toothpick inserted in center comes out clean. Remove from oven and let cool in pan.

6. Meanwhile, *prepare Strawberry Rhubarb Mousse:* In a saucepan, combine rhubarb, sugar and 2 tbsp (30 mL) water. Simmer, stirring constantly, until rhubarb is tender. Purée mixture in blender. Blend in strawberries, sour cream and cream cheese until smooth. Pour into a large bowl and set aside.

7. In a small bowl, sprinkle gelatin over 2 tbsp (30 mL) water; allow to stand for 1 minute. Add 2 tbsp (30 mL) boiling water, stirring constantly until gelatin completely dissolves. Stir dissolved gelatin into strawberry and rhubarb mixture.

8. In a separate, clean bowl, with clean beaters, beat egg whites until stiff but not dry and gradually beat in icing sugar. Fold stiff egg whites into strawberry and rhubarb mixture. Set aside.

9. Remove sponge cake from pan. Cut cake in half horizontally. Spread bottom layer with Rhubarb and Strawberry Mousse and cover with top layer. Place cake back into pan and refrigerate overnight.

10. *Prepare Cream Cheese Icing:* In a medium bowl, whip cream cheese, butter, icing sugar and vanilla until creamy.

11. Once cake is chilled and mousse is set, remove cake from pan and spread with Cream Cheese Icing.

Almond Butterscotch Bars

TIP: For the topping, try one of the trendy sugars, such as muscovado.

These bars are one of life's simple pleasures. They remind me of the Ladies' Auxiliary Teas they used to have when I was little—a real comfort food served with a cup of tea.

Makes 24 bars

Preheat oven to 350°F (180°C)
13- × 9-inch (3 L) baking pan, greased

1¹/₂ cups	all-purpose flour	375 mL
2 tsp	baking powder	10 mL
¹/₂ cup	butter	125 mL
2 cups	packed brown sugar	500 mL
2	eggs	2
1¹/₂ tsp	vanilla	7 mL
1 oz	semi-sweet chocolate	30 g

Nutty Topping

¹/₄ cup	butter	50 mL
¹/₃ cup	sugar	75 mL
¹/₃ cup	corn syrup	75 mL
¹/₄ tsp	salt	1 mL
1¹/₂ cups	sliced almonds	375 mL

1. In a small bowl, combine flour and baking powder; set aside.
2. Melt butter in a large saucepan. Remove from heat; blend in brown sugar. Beat in eggs and vanilla. Stir in flour mixture.
3. Spread batter in prepared pan. Bake in preheated oven for 20 minutes.
4. Meanwhile, *prepare Nutty Topping:* Melt butter in small saucepan. Mix in sugar, corn syrup, 2 tbsp (30 mL) water and salt. Bring mixture to a boil; boil for 4 minutes, stirring constantly. Stir in sliced almonds.
5. Spread Nutty Topping evenly over the surface of the cake. Continue baking for 15 minutes longer. Cool in pan for at least 60 minutes.
6. Melt chocolate in the microwave or in a small saucepan and drizzle over pan. Cut into bars.

Strawberry Trifle

Every cook deserves one recipe using convenience foods—this is yours.

Serves 6

1	package (3.5 oz/102 g) vanilla instant pudding mix	1
2 cups	milk	500 mL
1 cup	vanilla yogurt	250 mL
1	package (10 oz/298 g) frozen pound cake, thawed	1
	Strawberry jam for spreading	
1	package (15 oz/425 g) frozen sweetened strawberries,	
thawed	1	
1 cup	35% cream, whipped	250 mL
	sliced toasted almonds for garnish	

1. Prepare pudding mix according to package directions, using 2 cups (500 mL) milk. Stir in yogurt; set aside.

2. Cut cake into 12 slices. Spread jam over 6 slices; top with remaining 6 slices. Cut slices into cubes. Place cubes in bottom of a 6-cup (1.5 L) clear bowl.

3. Drain strawberries, reserving ¼ cup (50 mL) syrup. Sprinkle syrup over cake cubes; top with drained strawberries.

4. Pour pudding mixture over fruit in bowl. Cover and chill for at least 2 hours, or overnight. To serve, garnish with whipped cream and sliced almonds.

Variation

Substitute 4 cups (1 L) of fresh strawberries for the frozen strawberries. To replace the syrup from the frozen strawberries, use ¼ cup (50 mL) strawberry jelly, melted, or ¼ cup (50 mL) strawberry jam, melted and pressed through a sieve.

PER SERVING	
Calories	538
Protein (g)	8.2
Carbohydrates (g)	72.8
Fat (g)	25.3
Sat	12.4
Mono	9.6
Poly	1.7

TOP 10		
1	Calcium (mg)	220
2	Potassium (mg)	345
3	Vitamin D (µg)	1.3
4	Magnesium (mg)	32
5	Vitamin A (RE)	225
6	B_{12} (µg)	0.62
7	Zinc (mg)	0.8
8	Thiamin (mg)	0.14
9	Riboflavin (mg)	0.46
10	Niacin (NE)	2.65

Fresh Fruit Pizza

PER SERVING	
Calories	196
Protein (g)	5.1
Carbohydrates (g)	26.4
Fat (g)	8.1
Sat	2.8
Mono	3.4
Poly	1

TOP 10		
1	Calcium (mg)	89
2	Potassium (mg)	265
3	Vitamin D (μg)	0.6
4	Magnesium (mg)	22
5	Vitamin A (RE)	64
6	B_{12} (μg)	0.24
7	Zinc (mg)	0.5
8	Thiamin (mg)	0.11
9	Riboflavin (mg)	0.24
10	Niacin (NE)	1.87

TIP: You can substitute any type of fruit you prefer into this recipe.

Okay, so I'm stretching the definition of pizza a little. This recipe is easy and impressive . . . not to mention nutritious.

Serves 8

Preheat oven to 325°F (160°C)

1	ready-made 9" (23 cm) pie crust, baked	1
3	eggs, beaten	4
1/3 cup	granulated sugar	80 mL
Pinch	salt	Pinch
1 tsp	vanilla	5 mL
1 1/2 cups	milk	375 mL
2	Fresh kiwis, thinly sliced	2
1 cup	Fresh strawberries, thinly sliced	250 mL
2	Fresh oranges, thinly sliced	2

1. Preheat oven to 325°F (160°C).

2. In a medium bowl, mix together eggs, sugar, salt and vanilla.

3. Heat milk in microwave oven at high for 1½ minutes.

4. Whisk hot milk to egg mixture and whip. Pour into crust and bake in preheated oven for 40 minutes. Remove from oven. Cool. Arrange slices of the 3 fruits in an overlapping circular pattern. Chill thoroughly and enjoy!

Fabulous Rice Pudding

When I was a kid I hated rice pudding. If only Mom had known about the cream—it makes all the difference. Yes, it adds a few calories, but with the cream you get CLA (conjugated linoleic acid), plus a divine creaminess!

Serves 6

3 cups	milk	750 mL
1 cup	whipping (35%) cream	250 mL
1/2 cup	short-grain rice (Arborio or Italian-style)	125 mL
1/4 cup	packed brown sugar	50 mL
1/2 tsp	ground cinnamon	2 mL
1/4 tsp	salt	1 mL
1/4 cup	raisins (optional)	50 mL
1 tbsp	vanilla	15 mL

1. In a heavy saucepan, bring milk, whipping cream, rice, brown sugar, cinnamon and salt to boil over medium heat, stirring often. Reduce heat to low; cover and simmer, stirring occasionally, for 20 minutes.

2. Stir in raisins, if using. Cover and simmer, stirring occasionally, for 5 minutes longer, or until rice is very tender. Stir in vanilla. Serve warm or cold.

PER SERVING	
Calories	286
Protein (g)	6
Carbohydrates (g)	29.6
Fat (g)	16.3
Sat	10.1
Mono	4.7
Poly	0.6

TOP 10		
1	Calcium (mg)	185
2	Potassium (mg)	266
3	Vitamin D (µg)	1.3
4	Magnesium (mg)	26
5	Vitamin A (RE)	187
6	B_{12} (µg)	0.15
7	Zinc (mg)	0.8
8	Thiamin (mg)	0.05
9	Riboflavin (mg)	0.26
10	Niacin (NE)	1.68

TIP: This pudding thickens upon cooling. Add more cream or milk when serving to thin, if desired. Also, try dried cranberries instead of raisins.

Honey Almond Cake

This is an unassuming little cake, but it's easy to make and has added calcium from the milk and almonds.

Serves 10

Preheat oven to 350°F (180°C)
9-inch (2.5 L) square baking pan, buttered

1/2 cup	butter, softened	125 mL
1/2 cup	lightly packed brown sugar	125 mL
2	eggs, beaten	2
2 tbsp	liquid honey	30 mL
1 tbsp	almond extract	15 mL
1 1/2 cups	all-purpose flour	375 mL
1 tsp	baking powder	5 mL
1/2 cup	milk	125 mL
	Whole almonds	

Honey and Cream Cheese Icing

3 tbsp	butter	45 mL
4 oz	cream cheese, softened	125 g
2 tbsp	liquid honey, warmed	30 mL
3 tbsp	confectioner's (icing) sugar	45 mL

1. In a large bowl, cream butter with brown sugar. Beat in eggs, honey and almond extract. Set aside.

2. In a small bowl, mix flour with baking powder. Beat into butter mixture, alternately with milk, making 2 additions of each. Mix well until smooth.

3. Pour mixture into prepared pan and bake in preheated oven for 45 minutes or until knife or toothpick inserted in center comes out clean. Cool for 15 minutes in the pan.

4. While cake is cooling, *prepare Honey and Cream Cheese Icing:* In bowl, mix butter and cream cheese until smooth. Beat in honey and icing sugar. Keep in refrigerator until using.

5. When cake is cool, remove it from the pan, and top with Honey and Cream Cheese Icing, smoothing with a spatula. Garnish with whole almonds.

Amazing Berries 'n' Cream Mille Feuille

Don't let the phyllo dough frighten you; it's not that difficult. The hard part for me was learning to say "Mille Foy!"

Serves 6

Preheat oven to 400°F (220°C)
Large baking sheet

2 cups	frozen raspberries	500 mL
3 tbsp	confectioner's (icing) sugar	45 mL
2 tbsp	butter, melted	30 mL
4	sheets phyllo pastry dough	4
3/4 cup	whipping (35%) cream	200 mL
1 cup	vanilla yogurt	250 mL

PER SERVING	
Calories	251
Protein (g)	3.9
Carbohydrates (g)	23.8
Fat (g)	16.2
Sat	9.6
Mono	4.9
Poly	0.8

TOP 10		
1	Calcium (mg)	85
2	Potassium (mg)	159
3	Vitamin D (µg)	0.5
4	Magnesium (mg)	19
5	Vitamin A (RE)	163
6	B_{12} (µg)	0.24
7	Zinc (mg)	0.5
8	Thiamin (mg)	0.13
9	Riboflavin (mg)	0.22
10	Niacin (NE)	1.72

1. Thaw raspberries in a large shallow bowl. Sift 2 tbsp (30 mL) of the icing sugar over raspberries.

2. Butter each sheet of dough. Stack sheets up, one on top of the other, and sift remaining sugar over top. Cut dough into 18 roughly equal rectangles: slice dough lengthwise into thirds, then slice each third into 6 equal sections.

3. Place rectangles on baking sheet. Bake in preheated oven for 3 to 4 minutes, until golden. Cool.

4. Whip cream until stiff. Fold in yogurt. Refrigerate for up to 24 hours if not assembling right away.

5. *Assembly:* Place one pastry rectangle on each of 6 plates, cover with whipped cream mixture and dot with raspberries. Repeat, making another layer, and finish with pastry. Use raspberry liquid to decorate plate. Serve immediately.

Beverages

Frulatte

Mochaccino Cooler

Honey Orange Milkshake

Berry Blast

Choco-Strawberry Smoothie

Cranberry Splash

Peachy Orange Blossom

Tropical Sunshine

Frulatte

PER SERVING	
Calories	212
Protein (g)	8
Carbohydrates (g)	30.1
Fat (g)	7.6
Sat	4.5
Mono	2
Poly	0.4

TOP 10		
1	Calcium (mg)	277
2	Potassium (mg)	539
3	Vitamin D (μg)	1.9
4	Magnesium (mg)	44
5	Vitamin A (RE)	151
6	B$_{12}$ (μg)	0.8
7	Zinc (mg)	1.1
8	Thiamin (mg)	0.12
9	Riboflavin (mg)	0.45
10	Niacin (NE)	2.49

TIP: Frozen fruit works well also, and doubles the cooling effect

There's nothing to equal the cooling power of this drink. It's better than air-conditioning on a hot summer's day.

Serves 1

3/4 cup	milk	175 mL
3/4 cup	fresh fruit (strawberries, raspberries, blueberries or bananas)	175 mL
1/4 cup	vanilla ice cream	50 mL
1	ice cube (optional)	1

1. Combine milk and remaining ingredients in blender. Cover and blend at high speed until smooth. Serve immediately.

Mochaccino Cooler

You can eliminate the chocolate sauce to cut down on the calories—or share it with a friend! Of course, if you leave out the chocolate, it's not mocha anymore, is it? An excellent source of calcium.

Serves 1

2 tsp	instant coffee	10 mL
2 tsp	hot water	10 mL
3/4 cup	milk	175 mL
1/2 cup	vanilla ice cream	125 mL
2 tbsp	chocolate sauce	30 mL

1. Dissolve instant coffee in hot water. Combine milk, coffee, ice cream and chocolate sauce in a blender. Cover and blend at high speed until smooth. Serve immediately.

PER SERVING	
Calories	365
Protein (g)	10.6
Carbohydrates (g)	49.7
Fat (g)	14.2
Sat	8.2
Mono	4.5
Poly	0.5

TOP 10		
1	Calcium (mg)	343
2	Potassium (mg)	678
3	Vitamin D (µg)	1.9
4	Magnesium (mg)	65
5	Vitamin A (RE)	183
6	B_{12} (µg)	1
7	Zinc (mg)	1.4
8	Thiamin (mg)	0.12
9	Riboflavin (mg)	0.55
10	Niacin (NE)	3.74

TIP: Decaffeinated coffee is a good choice in place of regular.

Honey Orange Milkshake

PER SERVING	
Calories	205
Protein (g)	6.5
Carbohydrates (g)	42.5
Fat (g)	2.7
Sat	1.5
Mono	0.7
Poly	0.1

TOP 10		
1	Calcium (mg)	254
2	Potassium (mg)	666
3	Vitamin D (µg)	1.3
4	Magnesium (mg)	43
5	Vitamin A (RE)	125
6	B₁₂ (µg)	0.44
7	Zinc (mg)	0.7
8	Thiamin (mg)	0.27
9	Riboflavin (mg)	0.31
10	Niacin (NE)	2.21

Oranges contribute calcium, along with vitamin C and other good stuff. An excellent source of calcium.

Serves 2

4	oranges, peeled and coarsely chopped	4
1 cup	milk	250 mL
2 tsp	liquid honey	10 mL
1/2 tsp	vanilla	2 mL
4	ice cubes	4
	Ground nutmeg (optional)	

1. Purée chopped oranges, milk, honey and vanilla in food processor or blender until smooth. With food processor or blender on low speed, add ice cubes, one at a time. Mix for 15 to 20 seconds. Pour mixture in tall glasses and top with sprinkling of ground nutmeg. Serve immediately.

TIP: Kiwi are another option for this delicious milkshake.

Berry Blast

This is one of my weapons in the fight against osteoporosis.

Serves 1

1 cup	cold milk	250 mL
1/2 cup	blueberries (fresh or frozen)	125 mL
3/4 cup	raspberry yogurt	175 mL

1. Blend all ingredients until smooth.

PER SERVING	
Calories	346
Protein (g)	15.8
Carbohydrates (g)	54.1
Fat (g)	7.8
Sat	4.7
Mono	2
Poly	0.2

TOP 10		
1	Calcium (mg)	524
2	Potassium (mg)	770
3	Vitamin D (µg)	2.5
4	Magnesium (mg)	60
5	Vitamin A (RE)	182
6	B_{12} (µg)	1.68
7	Zinc (mg)	2.1
8	Thiamin (mg)	0.21
9	Riboflavin (mg)	0.77
10	Niacin (NE)	3.24

TIP: To save calories, you could use a yogurt made with artificial sweetener. I often make this recipe with vanilla yogurt and peaches or cantaloupe.

Choco-Strawberry Smoothie

This is an excellent source of many nutrients, but just because it's liquid don't act as though it's calorie-free. It makes a great breakfast drink; have it along with a small bran muffin.

Serves 4

2 cups	chocolate milk	500 mL
2 cups	strawberry ice cream	500 mL
1 cup	frozen strawberries	250 mL
1	banana	1

1. Combine all ingredients in a blender. Cover and blend at high speed until smooth.

Cranberry Splash

All the good stuff you've read about cranberries is true. Blend them with milk and yogurt, and you've got a drink that's hard to beat. An excellent source of calcium.

Serves 2

1 cup	cold milk	250 mL
3/4 cup	frozen cranberry juice concentrate	175 mL
3/4 cup	strawberry yogurt	175 mL

1. Blend all ingredients until smooth.

PER SERVING	
Calories	357
Protein (g)	7.8
Carbohydrates (g)	74.2
Fat (g)	3.7
Sat	2.3
Mono	1
Poly	0.1

TOP 10		
1	Calcium (mg)	272
2	Potassium (mg)	406
3	Vitamin D (µg)	1.2
4	Magnesium (mg)	33
5	Vitamin A (RE)	91
6	B_{12} (µg)	0.84
7	Zinc (mg)	1.1
8	Thiamin (mg)	0.11
9	Riboflavin (mg)	0.4
10	Niacin (NE)	1.53

TIP: For a really interesting drink, try this with one of the cultured milks, such as Kefir.

Peachy Orange Blossom

Blending milk and/or yogurt with a variety of fruits and juices is a great way to increase your servings of these two important (and under-consumed) food groups. If you pair one of these drinks with a high-fiber muffin, you've got yourself a good start to the day. An excellent source of calcium.

Serves 2

1 cup	cold milk	250 mL
1 cup	peach yogurt	250 mL
1/2 cup	mandarin oranges, drained	125 mL
1/4 cup	orange juice	50 mL

1. Blend all ingredients until smooth. Serve cold.

Tropical Sunshine

With so many frozen juice concentrates available now, you can whip up any number of combinations. Mango or papaya can easily replace the pineapple.

Serves 2

1 tbsp	frozen orange juice concentrate	15 mL
1/2 cup	crushed pineapple	125 mL
1 1/2 cups	cold milk	375 mL

1. Blend orange juice concentrate and pineapple in a blender. Add milk. Cover and blend until smooth.

PER SERVING	
Calories	**142**
Protein (g)	**6.6**
Carbohydrates (g)	**22**
Fat (g)	**3.6**
Sat	2.2
Mono	0.9
Poly	0.1

TOP 10		
1	Calcium (mg)	234
2	Potassium (mg)	418
3	Vitamin D (µg)	1.9
4	Magnesium (mg)	37
5	Vitamin A (RE)	109
6	B_{12} (µg)	0.67
7	Zinc (mg)	0.8
8	Thiamin (mg)	0.15
9	Riboflavin (mg)	0.32
10	Niacin (NE)	1.89

TIP: You can't do yourself a better favor than to increase your intake of milk products and fruits and vegetables. These drink combos are an easy way to do just that.

Bibliography

Calcium

Abrams, S.A. "Calcium Turnover and Nutrition Through the Life Cycle." *Proceedings of the Nutrition Society* 60, no. 2 (2001): 283–89.

Baker, S.S., W.J. Cochran, C.A. Flores, M.K. Georgieff, M.S. Jacobson, T. Jaksic, and N.F. Krebs (American Academy of Pediatrics, Committee on Nutrition). "Calcium Requirements of Infants, Children, and Adolescents." *Pediatrics* 104, no. 5, part 1 (1999): 1152–57.

Black, R.E., S.M. Williams, I.E. Jones, and A. Goulding. "Children Who Avoid Drinking Cow Milk Have Low Dietary Calcium Intakes and Poor Bone Health." *American Journal of Clinical Nutrition* 76, no. 3 (2002): 675–80.

Bonjour, J.P., A.L. Carrie, S. Ferrari, H. Clavien, D. Slosman, G. Theintz, and R. Rizzoli. "Calcium-Enriched Foods and Bone Mass Growth in Prepubertal Girls: A Randomized, Double-Blind, Placebo-Controlled Trial." *Journal of Clinical Investigation* 99, no. 6 (1997): 1287–94.

Bucher, H.C., R.J. Cook, G.H. Guyatt, J.D. Lang, D.J. Cook, R. Hatala, and D.L. Hunt. "Effects of Dietary Calcium Supplementation on Blood Pressure. A Meta-Analysis of Randomized Controlled Trials." *Journal of the American Medical Association* 275, no. 13 (1996): 1016–22.

Chapuy, M.C., M.E Arlot, F. Duboeuf, J. Brun, B. Crouzet, S. Arnaud, P.D. Delmas, and P.J. Meunier. "Vitamin D_3 and Calcium to Prevent Hip Fractures in Elderly Women." New England Journal of Medicine 327 (1992): 1637–42.

Curhan, G.C., W.C. Willett, F.E. Speizer, D. Spiegelman, and M.J. Stampfer. "Comparison of Dietary Calcium with Supplemental Calcium and Other Nutrients as Factors Affecting the Risk for Kidney Stones in Women." *Annals of Internal Medicine* 26, no. 7 (1997): 497–504.

Dawson-Hughes, B., and S.S. Harris. "Calcium Intake Influences the Association of Protein Intake with Rates of Bone Loss in Elderly Men and Women." *American Journal of Clinical Nutrition* 75, no. 4 (2002): 773–79.

Goodman, M.T., A.H. Wu, K.H. Tung, K. McDuffie, L.N. Kolonel, A.M. Nomura, K. Terada, L.R. Wilkens, S. Murphy, and J.H. Hankin. "Association of Dairy Products, Lactose, and Calcium with the Risk of Ovarian Cancer." *American Journal of Epidemiology* 156, no. 2 (2002): 148–57.

Gueguen, L., and A. Pointillart. "The Bioavailability of Dietary Calcium." *Journal of the American College of Nutrition* 19, no. 2, supplement (2000): 119–36S.

Heaney, R.P. "Calcium, Dairy Products and Osteoporosis." *Journal of the American College of Nutrition* 19, no.2, supplement (2000): 83–99S.

Heaney, R.P. "Calcium Needs of the Elderly to Reduce Fracture Risk." *Journal of the American College of Nutrition* 20, no. 2, supplement (2001): 192–97S.

Heaney, R.P. "The Importance of Calcium Intake for Lifelong Skeletal Health." *Calcified Tissue International* 70, no. 2 (2002): 70–73.

Heaney, R.P. "Thinking Straight About Calcium." *New England Journal of Medicine* 328, no. 7 (1993): 503–5.

Heaney, R.P., K.M. Davies, and M.J. Barger-Lux. "Calcium and Weight: Clinical Studies." *Journal of the American College of Nutrition* 21, no. 2, supplement (2002): 152–55S.

Hu J.F., X.H. Zhao, J.B. Jia, B. Parpia, and T.C. Campbell. "Dietary Calcium and Bone Density Among Middle-Aged and Elderly Women in China." *American Journal of Clinical Nutrition* 58, no. 2 (1993): 219–27.

Martin, A.D., D.A. Bailey, H.A. McKay, and S. Whiting. "Bone Mineral and Calcium Accretion During Puberty." *American Journal of Clinical Nutrition* 66 (1997): 611–15.

Moynihan, P.J., S. Ferrier, and G.N. Jenkins. "The Cariostatic Potential of Cheese: Cooked Cheese-Containing Meals Increase Plaque Calcium Concentration." *British Dental Journal* 187, no. 12 (1999): 664–67.

New, S.A. "Calcium, Protein, and Fruit and Vegetables as Dietary Determinants of Bone Health." *American Journal of Clinical Nutrition* 77 (2003): 1340–41.

Osteoporosis Society of Canada. "Consensus on Calcium Nutrition (1993): Official Position of the Osteoporosis Society of Canada." *Nutrition Quarterly* 18, no. 3 (1994): 62–69.

Recker, R.R. "Prevention of Osteoporosis: Calcium Nutrition." *Osteoporosis International* 1, supplement (1993): S163–65.

Roughead, Z.K., L.K. Johnson, G.I. Lykken, and J.R. Hunt. "Controlled High Meat Diets Do Not Affect Calcium Retention or Indices of Bone Status in Healthy Postmenopausal Women." *Journal of Nutrition* 133, no. 4 (2003): 20–26.

Teegarden, D., R.M. Lyle, G.P. McCabe, L.D. McCabe, W.R. Proulx, K. Michon, A.P. Knight, C.C. Johnston, and C.M. Weaver. "Dietary Calcium, Protein and Phosphorus Are Related to Bone Mineral Density and Content in Young Women." *American Journal of Clinical Nutrition* 68, no. 3 (1998): 749–54.

Thys-Jacob, S. "Micronutrients and the Premenstrual Syndrome: The Case for Calcium." *Journal of the American College of Nutrition* 19, no. 2 (2000): 220–27.

Weaver, C.M. "Calcium Nutrition: Strategies for Maximal Bone Mass." *Journal of Women's Health* 6, no. 6 (1997): 661–64.

Weaver, C.M., and K.L. Plawecki. "Dietary Calcium: Adequacy of a Vegetarian Diet." *American Journal of Clinical Nutrition* 59, supplement (1994): 1238–41S.

Weaver, C.M., W.R. Proulx, and R. Heaney. "Choices for Achieving Adequate Dietary Calcium with a Vegetarian Diet." *American Journal of Clinical Nutrition* 70, no. 3, supplement (1999): 543–48S.

Zemel, M.B. "Regulation of Adiposity and Obesity Risk by Dietary Calcium: Mechanisms and Implications." *Journal of the American College of Nutrition* 21, no. 2, supplement (2002): 146–51S.

Calcium and Colon Cancer

Baron, J.A., M. Beach, J.S. Mandel, R.U. van Stolk, R.W. Haile, R.S. Sandler, R. Rothstein, R.W. Summers, D.C. Snover, G.J. Beck, J.H. Bond, and E.R. Greenberg (Calcium Polyp Prevention Study Group). "Calcium Supplements for the Prevention of Colorectal Adenomas." *New England Journal of Medicine* 340, no. 2 (1999): 101–7.

Buset, M. "Colorectal Cancer and Dietary Calcium: A Word of Hope." *European Journal of Cancer Prevention* 2, no. 2 (1993): 187–88.

Holt, P.R. "Dairy Foods and Prevention of Colon Cancer: Human Studies." *Journal of the American College of Nutrition* 18, no. 5, supplement (1999): 379–91S.

Hyman, J., J.A. Baron, B.J. Dain, R.S. Sandler, R.W. Haile, J.S. Mandel, L.A. Mott, and E.R. Greenberg. "Dietary and Supplemental Calcium and the Recurrence of Colorectal Adenomas." *Cancer Epidemiology Biomarkers and Prevention* 7, no. 4 (1998): 291–95.

Jarvinen, R., P. Knekt, T. Hakulinen, and A. Aromaa. "Prospective Study on Milk Products, Calcium and Cancers of the Colon and Rectum." *European Journal of Clinical Nutrition* 55, no. 11 (2001):1000–1007.

Martinez, M.E., E.L. Giovannucci, G.A. Colditz, M.J. Stampfer, D.J. Hunter, F.E. Speizer, A. Wing, and W.C. Willett. "Calcium, Vitamin D and the Occurrence of Colorectal Cancer Among Women." *Journal of the National Cancer Institute* 88, no. 19 (1996): 1375–82.

McCullough, M.L., A.S Robertson, C. Rodriguez, E.J. Jacobs, A. Chao, J. Carolyn, E.E. Calle, W.C. Willett, and M.J. Thun. "Calcium, Vitamin D, Dairy Products and Risk of Colorectal Cancer in the Cancer Prevention Study II Nutrition Cohort (United States)." *Cancer Causes Control* 14, no. 1 (2003): 1–12.

Terry, P., J.A. Baron, L. Bergkvist, L. Holmberg, and A. Wolk. "Dietary Calcium and Vitamin D Intake and Risk of Colorectal Cancer: A Prospective Cohort Study in Women." *Nutrition and Cancer* 43, no. 1 (2002): 39–46.

Wu, K., W.C. Willett, C.S. Fuchs, G.A. Colditz, and E.L. Giovannucci. "Calcium Intake and Risk of Colon Cancer in Women and Men." *Journal of the National Cancer Institute* 94, no. 6 (2002): 437–46.

Calcium and Heart Disease

Al-Delaimy, W.K., E. Rimm, W.C. Willett, M.J. Stampfer, and F.B. Hu. "A Prospective Study of Calcium Intake from Diet and Supplements and Risk of Ischemic Heart Disease Among Men." *American Journal of Clinical Nutrition* 77 (2003): 814–18.

Bucher, H.C., R.J. Cook, G.H. Guyatt, J.D. Lang, D.J. Cook, R. Hatala, and D.L. Hunt. "Effects of Dietary Calcium Supplementation on Blood Pressure: A Meta-Analysis of Randomized Controlled Trials." *Journal of the American Medical Association* 275, no. 13 (1996): 1016–22.

Griffith, L.E, G.H. Guyatt, R.J. Cook, H.C. Bucher, and D.J. Cook. "The Influence of Dietary and Nondietary Calcium Supplementation on Blood Pressure: An Updated Meta-Analysis of Randomized Controlled Trials." *American Journal of Hypertension* 12 (1999): 84–92.

McCarron, D.A., and M.E. Reusser. "Finding Consensus in the Dietary Calcium-Blood Pressure Debate." *Journal of the American College of Nutrition* 18, no. 5, supplement (1999): 398–405S.

Calcium and Kidney Stones

Curhan, G.C. "Dietary Calcium, Dietary Protein and Kidney Stone Formation." *Mineral and Electrolyte Metabolism* 23, nos. 3–6 (1997): 261–64.

Curhan, G.C., W.C. Willett, E.B. Rimm, M.J. Stampfer. "A Prospective Study of Dietary Calcium and Other Nutrients and the Risk of Symptomatic Kidney Stones." *New England Journal of Medicine* 328, no. 12 (1993): 833–38.

Stern, R. "Calcium and Kidney Stones." *New England Journal of Medicine* 329, no. 7 (1993): 509.

Vitamin D

Abrams, S.A. "Nutritional Rickets: An Old Disease Returns." *Nutrition Reviews* 60, no. 4 (2002): 111–15.

Bishop, N. "Rickets Today: Children Still Need Milk and Sunshine." *New England Journal of Medicine* 341, no. 8 (1999): 602–4.

Carvalho, N.F., R.D. Kenney, P.H. Carrington, and D.E. Hall. "Severe Nutritional Deficiencies in Toddlers Resulting from Health Food Milk Alternatives." *Pediatrics* 107, no. 4 (2001): E46.

Gloth, F.M. 3rd, C.M. Gundberg, B.W. Hollis, J.G. Haddad Jr., and J.D. Tobin. "Vitamin D Deficiency in Homebound Elderly Persons." *Journal of the American Medical Association* 274, no. 21 (1995): 1683–86.

Heaney, R.P., and C.M. Weaver. "Calcium and Vitamin D." *Endocrinology and Metabolism Clinics of North America* 32 (2003): 181–94.

Holick, M.F. "Environmental Factors That Influence the Cutaneous Production of Vitamin D." *American Journal of Clinical Nutrition* 61, no. 3, supplement (1995): 638–45S.

Holick, M.F. "McCollum Award Lecture, 1994: Vitamin D—New Horizons for the 21st Century." *American Journal of Clinical Nutrition* 60 (1994): 619–30.

Lehtonen-Veromaa, M.K., T.T. Mottonen, I.O. Nuotio, K.M. Irjala, A.E. Leino, and J.S. Viikari. "Vitamin D and Attainment of Peak Bone Mass Among Peripubertal Finnish Girls: A 3-Y Prospective Study." *American Journal of Clinical Nutrition* 76, no. 6 (2002): 1446–53.

Lesser, G.T. "Vitamin D Deficiency in Women with Hip Fracture." *Journal of the American Medical Association* 283, no. 11 (2000): 1425–26.

Pimlott, N.J., and M.F. Evans. "Regular Vitamin D Supplementation for Housebound, Frail Elderly People." *Canadian Family Physician* 43 (1997): 2127–28.

Rucker, D., J.A. Allan, G.H. Fick, and D.A. Hanley. "Vitamin D Insufficiency in a Population of Healthy Western Canadians." *Canadian Medical Association Journal* 166, no. 12 (2002): 1517–24.

Vieth, R. "Vitamin D Supplementation, 25-Hydroxyvitamin D Concentrations, and Safety." *American Journal of Clinical Nutrition* 69 (1999): 842–56.

Vieth, R., P.C. Chan, and G.D. MacFarlane. "Efficacy and Safety of Vitamin D_3 Intake Exceeding the Lowest Observed Adverse Effect Level." *American Journal of Clinical Nutrition* 73, no. 2 (2001): 288–94.

Vieth, R., D.E. Cole, G.A. Hawker, H.M. Trang, and L.A. Rubin. "Wintertime Vitamin D Insufficiency Is Common in Young Canadian Women, and Their Vitamin D Intake Does Not Prevent It." *European Journal of Clinical Nutrition* 55, no. 12 (2001): 1091–97.

Vieth, R., and D. Fraser. "Vitamin D Insufficiency: No Recommended Dietary Allowance Exists for This Nutrient." *Canadian Medical Association Journal* 166, no. 12 (2002): 1541–42.

Index

The Everyday Calcium Cookbook

Other Healthy Living Cookbooks by Key Porter Books

The New Lighthearted Cookbook by Anne Lindsay
Endorsed by the Heart and Stroke Foundation

The Migraine Cookbook by Michele Sharp
Endorsed by the Migraine Association of Canada
And Winner of the Gourmand World Cookbook Awards
For Best Health and Nutrition Book

The Everyday Dairy-Free Cookbook
by Miller Rogers and Emily White

HeartHealthy Cooking
Edited by Bridget Wilson and Barbara Ledermann
Endorsed by Becel

The Everyday Wheat-Free & Gluten-Free Cookbook
by Michelle Berriedale-Johnson
Endorsed by the Canadian Celiac Association

*For more information, please visit *www.keyporter.com*